Coming Up from Down in the Dumps

Coming Up from Down in the Dumps

Afton Day

Bookcraft
Salt Lake City, Utah

Copyright © 1986 by Bookcraft, Inc.

All rights reserved. This book or any part thereof may not be reproduced in any form whatsoever, whether by graphic, visual, electronic, filming, microfilming, tape recording, or any other means, without the prior written permission of Bookcraft, Inc., except in the case of brief passages embodied in critical reviews and articles.

Library of Congress Catalog Card Number: 86-70650
ISBN 0-88494-597-9

First Printing, 1986

Printed in the United States of America

Contents

	Preface	vii
1	Call It What You Like, but Deal with It	1
2	Space	13
3	We Are Driven	23
4	What in the Dickens Is Wrong with Great Expectations?	39
5	Kid Burnout: The Problem	50
6	Kid Burnout: The Solution	66
7	Shall the Youth of Zion Flicker?	81
8	The Enlightened Mind	101
9	How to Prevent Being the Burner	111
10	Getting Started	121

Preface

I fully intend to write my next book on some frivolous subject, like *Creative Candle Dipping* or *How to Live on $200,000 a Year.* It seems that whenever I write about a real-people problem, I have to prove that I can overcome the problem myself before I can speak with authority. You can see why I don't write about axe-murderers or zombies.

My own burnout began nearly ten years ago, and, although I should have known better, I let it generalize. I've experienced nearly every kind of burnout I describe in this book, except possibly kid burnout and missionary burnout. (I'm safe on one account. They can make me a missionary, but they can't make me a kid again.) After much spiritual restructuring I can honestly say that I love my job. I can even admit that I'm happy in my Church calling, and when you consider that I, who break out in a rash at the mere mention of embroidery floss and Elmer's Glue, am serving as homemaking leader, that's an accomplishment. I still fluctuate between serene spouse and paranoid partner, and between pleasant parent and martyr mother, but I guess that's to be expected. Maybe it was intended that the eternal occupations would take longer to master.

Burnout is, I guess, a fad expression and, as such, is suspect to some. I grew to dread the friendly conversation-starter, "What book are you working on now?" While some people expressed delight that I was exposing a widespread and potentially devastating condition, others were shocked, even angry, that I would lend credibility to what they saw as a common cop-out. Many people insisted that while "the world" might suffer burnout, Mormons didn't; others saw burnout as a weak excuse to get out of taking responsibility.

Like it or not, burnout is real, even among Latter-day Saints. Ignoring it won't help. It can be overcome, and it can be prevented, but only by positive action, not by denial. When you get down to the nitty-gritty, it's true that the way we prevent burnout is the same way we prevent (or overcome) depression, alcoholism, obesity, or whatever else may be standing between where we are now and where we want to be —by living the gospel of Christ. Most of us who have become sidetracked need a gentle nudge in the right direction. It's this nudge, along with some experiences and information that you will possibly be able to identify with, that I offer in this book.

Call It What You Like, but Deal with It

1

It was a typical kindergarten day in the seven-room schoolhouse in a small Utah town. The children, having known only Primary and Sunday School teachers, insisted on calling me, the new teacher, "Sister Day," and for show and tell Tiffany Tingey sang "I Am a Child of God" and Harold Folsom told about his sister's recent wedding reception at the ward meetinghouse across the street. But the comfortable, churchlike atmosphere changed when it became evident that Levi Smith had learned his first swearword.

Having obviously used the word on his family with most gratifying results, Levi repeatedly wove the shocking word into his speech with a proficiency that would shame the best paperback novel writer. None of us failed him. The teachers, the principal, the other children, and especially the school secretary, who was also the stake president's wife, rewarded him with looks of horror and excited tongue lashings whenever he spoke the word. Shy little Levi was a star that day.

I've discovered a way to get an excited response from others without resorting to verbal obscenities. I just say the word *burnout!* Nobody can hear that word and remain unemotional. In the short distance it takes to walk from Sears to

Penney's in the mall I've heard about job burnout, marriage burnout, college-student burnout, and creativity burnout. Just walking from the chapel to the Relief Society room I've been introduced to parent burnout, high school—student burnout (also called the Senior Slump), church job burnout, and missionary burnout. With the exception of a fortunate few everyone has experienced burnout in some form or another.

While most people respond to the mention of the word with heartrending stories and personal examples, a few—usually business executives or school administrators—react violently. Burnout, they say, is a cop-out. "It's like stress," said one. "It's a fad expression, and people use it as an excuse to mope, to complain, and, in general, do less than their best."

Which responses do I respond to? All of the above. The problem I discovered when I set about to gather information for this book is that, because "burnout" is a recently coined label, it can't be neatly packaged. Those who have experienced it or are currently experiencing it have one reaction, "Yes, it should be exposed for what it is: a disturbing, sometimes overwhelming, state of limbo," while those who have seen it in a family member or employee often *do* see it as an excuse, a cop-out, or a passing fad. This is due, I believe, partly to the fact that people use the *condition* (burnout) to excuse an irresponsible way of *handling the condition*.

To explain this, I'll give a brief introduction to some of the many kinds of burnout which any of us might experience. Let it be known that I give credibility to all kinds of burnout. If it occurs, it's worth knowing about. That is *not* to say that I lend respectability to all ways of *handling* burnout. Marriage burnout, for example. I contend that marriage burnout exists. I've read about it, I've heard about it, I've seen it, I may even have experienced it in a mild form. I recognize the term *marriage burnout* and I accept that some, not all, people suffer from its symptoms. But just because I believe in marriage burnout does not mean that I condone leaving your mate and your kids and joining a computer dating service. The label *burnout* describes the feelings of discouragement, despair, and discontent suffered by the disheartened wife or husband. The way the burnout is handled is a different matter entirely. It is

Call It What You Like, but Deal with It   3

my hope, in writing this book, to offer constructive options which lessen the necessity of reacting to burnout in the frenzied, irrational ways that have obviously joined the phrase *burnout* with irresponsibility, weakness, and whiners.

The term *burnout* elicits a mind-set. While one person may be enthusiastically ready to jump on the job burnout band-wagon, the same person may be completely baffled at the idea of marriage burnout, wondering what on earth the two conditions could possibly have in common. Another, deep in the throes of parent burnout, might respond with shock when I mention that some willful Saints might actually experience church job burnout. While I grow increasingly aware of the underlying similarities among all kinds of burnout, there seems to be a popular tendency to compartmentalize. Hopefully, when you finish this book you will see the common threads. To begin with, though, I'll give a short description of the most prominent types of burnout as I see them.

Job burnout (With a short *o*. It might be interesting to analyze the Job with a long *o* in terms of burnout, too!): Job burnout is quite common and very painful. It is common because most people have jobs; it is painful because most of us have to keep our jobs. The all-encompassing term *job burnout* means different things to different people: too much pressure, too little variety; too much work, too little self-direction. Your boss is too bossy; your boss is too wishy-washy. Responsible reactions to job burnout include reassessing your goals and talents and looking for a new job while still filling the requirements of your old one, reassessing your performance and goals in relationship to your present job and making constructive changes, and reassessing your expectations and reconstructing your attitude. An irresponsible way of handling job burnout is to one day announce that you've had enough and you're going to try expressionistic painting in the South Seas. Irresponsible unless, of course, you're independently wealthy or tremendously talented.

Marriage burnout: Considering (1) the huge discrepancy between the expectancy and the reality of marriage, (2) the expected longevity of the marriage relationship, and (3) the fact that individuals are constantly growing and changing, participants in the marriage relationship set themselves up for all kinds of challenges. Idealistic people may contend that burnout has set in when marriage becomes an everyday life-style instead of a torrid love affair. I, on the other hand, believe that marriage burnout can occur at any time during the relationship and it usually involves a serious, long-term change for the worse resulting from depression, low self-esteem, feelings of hopelessness, or feelings of stagnation in the burnee. Marriage burnout is difficult to handle because it almost always involves an element of blame which *seems* to preclude personal responsibility. There are three alternatives to marriage burnout: Get out of the marriage, muddle through, or make some initially difficult but potentially positive changes. Except in extreme cases I reject the first on the basis of kids, covenant, and commitment. I reject the second because muddling through is painful and stultifying, and tends to encourage "the blahs." I'll discuss some possible positive permutations in a later chapter.

Parent burnout: There are all levels of parent burnout, not the least of which is a harmless variety limited to mothers of large and longitudinal (spanning many years) families. These mothers, having already raised some children to adulthood (or close to it), discover that they've run out of steam for their still-to-be-contended-with "little kids." But that's okay. Because they don't have time to worry, feel guilty, read child-development books, or talk baby talk, these mothers treat their kids like normal human beings only to discover that they've created (I use the term loosely) well-adjusted, precocious little geniuses.

The people who really suffer from this mother's burnout are the PTA president, the little league auxiliary, and the ward nursery director. After twenty years of baby-sitting, ten years as a PTA officer, and sixteen seasons as somebody's team mother, she's had it! Let her send a cake or write a check or even just sit this one out sometime. She's earned a break.

Technically a condition doesn't meet my criteria for burnout unless it involves some pain and much frustration. Parent burnout, by definition, must include at least one "Where did I go wrong?" a smattering of "This is the thanks I get?" and an element of "What did I do to deserve this?"

Kid burnout: Kids are well known for their resilience, their durability, and above all, their youth. Burn out? Never! Then why do we occasionally get shaken from our comfortable sense of well-being by the dreadful headline announcing the suicide of the honor student / star athlete / all-round-popular-good kid? And what about those kids who constantly elicit "He's just lazy" from the frustrated teachers who can't figure out why, with an IQ like *that*, the potential *A* student hands in absolutely no work? Maybe I'm doing some pigeon-holing here, but it seems to me that we can learn something about childhood depression and the underachiever by looking at kids in terms of the burnout phenomenon.

Missionary burnout: I'm afraid that new missionaries often operate under the same misconceptions as do newlyweds: "Because you're approaching the best two years of your life, and because you will be engaged in the work of the Lord, life on the mission will be one big spiritual high. If it's not, something must be wrong with *you!*"

While I can't speak from personal experience, my observations lead me to believe that while a mission can, and ought to, provide some fantastic spiritual experiences, it is not without its share of pain, frustration, drudgery, and downright humiliation. (To one handsome young man I know, just having to admit that for all his irresistible charisma he *still* had to wash his own socks and underwear was humiliation enough!) Hopefully it helps to know that it's normal to feel like a mixed-up nineteen-year-old[1] sometimes, and that there are some things you can do to make your lows less low and the "nothing" days more tolerable and the "missionary experiences" start happening.

Church job burnout: In the Church most of us get opportunities to be the teacher and the student, the administrator and the board member, the burner and the burnee. The organization of the Church is, as I guess it was meant to be, an ideal network for the teaching and learning of human relations. Whether you "just can't get the spirit of your calling" or you're suffering an anxiety attack because you're trying to lead

---

1. Or whatever.

a group that won't follow, it's a never-ending struggle. Or, as your leadership trainer would say, a marvelous opportunity for growth.

We've attached several myths, or at least half-truths, to our ideas about Church jobs. One is that if you live righteously you can sit back and let the Lord do it for you. Another is that if you do your Church job admirably, the rest of your life will take care of itself. We think that "Church activity" and "living the gospel" are synonomous. Can we talk? Your Church calling can be an exciting and fulfilling part of your life, or it can be a thorn in your side. Or, you can use it to strengthen others or to become a thorn in someone else's side! Why do we burn out? How do we cause others to burn out? Stay tuned.

Now that we've talked about some specific kinds of burnout, I'd like to look at some common elements. We can best describe burnout at large by looking at (1) how it feels and (2) what it makes us do. I got my information from a variety of sources: other literature, open-ended questionnaires, personal interviews, and the School of Hard Knocks. Conveniently, in most cases, the questionnaires augmented the literature and the personal interviews supported the questionnaires. My personal experience affirmed them all, so in order to keep it simple I'll only cite specific sources when they shed a new light or when they add something I couldn't have possibly thought of myself.

The feelings most commonly associated with burnout are frustration, depression, grouchiness, the inability to be pleasant with family and friends, apathy, and anger. Most burned-out people direct their anger at an authority figure, usually "the boss." Some, especially those who feel that they cannot live up to their own expectations, are angry with themselves. Exhaustion, disillusionment, and indifference are feelings familiar to one in a burned-out state. Common responses to the question, "How did it feel to be burned out?" are: "I felt like totally giving up on everything." "I lost interest in life itself." "What's the purpose of all this?" "Why bother?" "I found myself giving a shoulder-shrugging response to a

Call It What You Like, but Deal with It 7

world which deserved much, much more from me." Herbert Freudenburger summed it up concisely in his observation that burnout is the feeling that there is something amiss between self and environment.[2] I've also heard burnout defined as the depletion of creative resources through exhaustion and a mismatch between effort and results.

While the majority of rekindled souls can look back on their burned-out selves and single out symptoms, most of us, while we are suffering, refuse to admit that there is anything wrong. Wrong with us, anyway. We become detached and cynical, and develop a skill for displacing the blame for our problems. The most common scapegoat is an employer or mate to whom we've given the power to thwart our creative talents, browbeat us, or "keep us in our places." Burned-out people usually follow a pattern of first becoming angry, then fighting, then giving up.

Burning out is nothing to be ashamed of, because most burnout victims come from the ranks of the high-achievement, success-oriented people. Easygoing, "laid back" people seldom suffer. While some Latter-day Saints have reached a spiritual plane where faith and serenity are well-developed character traits, the rest of us are highly susceptible to burnout. How can we not be, when we are constantly "encouraged" in our quest for perfection by reminders that where much is given, much is required, and by admonitions to remember who we are and what we represent? How many times I have sat in testimony meeting and heard someone state that they felt an awesome responsibility to carry on the great family name or to be a beacon light to all the nonmembers in their high school or office. All worthy goals, for sure, but tough taskmasters to the individual who has not learned to temper his attempts at being all things to all people with self-acceptance, trust, and patience.

Burnout nearly always starts in one specific area of our lives. If we are wise enough and honest enough to recognize it

---

2. Dr. Herbert J. Freudenberger, Ph.D., with Geraldine Richelson, *Burn Out: How to Beat the High Cost of Success* (New York: Doubleday and Company, 1980).

and uproot it, all is well. We can then add our name to those already in the Burnout Hall of Fame and go on with the task of living. Unfortunately, for many of us, the weaknesses that made us susceptible to burnout in the first place cause us to allow the condition to progress, and we find ourselves becoming more and more dismal and less and less effective. In other words, your job becomes increasingly tedious and unrewarding and you contract job burnout. You become negative and defeated, and your relationships at home suffer. The bogged-down feeling extends to your activities at Church. Before long you have job burnout, marriage burnout, parent burnout, and Church job burnout. If you're extremely thorough, as many burnout victims are, you may even develop neighborhood burnout and tennis court burnout. You know you're on dangerous ground when your plants die and your dog gets the mange. Your life as a whole becomes difficult and boring. You begin wondering why eternal life once sounded so good to you. The fifty or so more years you're expecting to live on this earth sound overwhelming enough, but—*eternity?*

I can name the exact date that my since-generalized burnout began to manifest itself. The groundwork had been laid years earlier, as I later discovered, but the symptoms surfaced when I pushed my way back onto full-time teaching after a greatly extended educational/maternity leave.

I mention the teaching profession only after weeks of asking myself "should I or shouldn't I?"—not wishing to center on the well-publicized and, some believe, overemphasized subject of teacher burnout specifically. While there are, I believe, some very obvious reasons that teachers are extremely susceptible, I've heard stories similar to mine from business executives, factory workers, and homemakers, so I share my experience in the hope that you can relate it to your own situation or to that of someone you know.

There was a sense of foreboding from the start. I was all dressed up and excited to have made it to the final interview. Still, when I stepped into that classroom I felt it closing in on me; I felt a sick, heavy feeling in the pit of my stomach that immediately made me wonder. Was this the feeling of dullness they talk about in Doctrine and Covenants 9:9? I feel a stupor of thought just trying to write about it!

It was an open classroom, which meant team teaching. Good news and bad news. Years ago "team teaching" had been the cry of the day, and I was chomping at the bit to try it. It had meant progress, adventure, growth. But the outline on the other side of the coin was distinct. While I'd always liked to think of myself as sociable and friendly, I was a loner when it came to work. I'd shuddered when professors assigned group projects, and to save my sanity I'd usually found a way to pacify my team members and do the work myself. My favorite qualities—spontaneity, nonconformity, and autonomy—were not necessarily the qualities of a good team member. I needed my space. But I told my doubts to be quiet. I'd never failed at anything I'd wanted to do before. What made me think I'd start now? I decided that if I got the job it was meant to be, and if I didn't, it wasn't. I did.

That year I learned the meaning of the word *insomnia*. Not that I couldn't get to sleep at night, by any means! By 10:00 P.M. my bed and I were inseparable. By 10:10 I swear I had hit the rapid eye movement stage. Exhaustion. But at 3:30 A.M. (exactly—my subconscious never ceases to amaze me, the way it can tell time in the dark!) I'd wake up with an almost intolerable sense of panic. Sometimes I could blame it on something, like the fear that my kids would grow up and say they would have turned out better but their mother never fixed them breakfast, or the certainty that the board of health would come and close down my house because of the constant mound of day-old food and grungy dishes which usually extended from the kitchen sink to the TV area. I sometimes catastrophized that my students wouldn't pass their quarterly tests, and I would be shunned as incompetent, unaccountable, and, like the naked emperor, stupid and unfit for my job. And sometimes the fear was present, but unaccounted for. It hurt as much either way.

The daytime hours weren't much better. I used to start my days by running in the darkness at 5:00 A.M. I can remember many times that year, running around the track, tears streaming down my face and a lump in my throat so constricting I could hardly breathe. I can remember sitting in church on Sunday (it seems that running and church provided the only time I had to think) and wondering not *Why me?* but simply, *Why?* At one time I had nearly convinced myself that the Lord had given me this challenge to teach me humility. But then I thought: *No, this isn't humility I'm feeling, it's pure humiliation. There's a difference.*

At this time teacher burnout was getting a lot of publicity but I thought the term couldn't possibly apply to me. I thought burnout was for people who had been at a job for years and had become stale. Later I discovered this wasn't the only requirement. (I'll analyze the causes of burnout in the next chapter; there can be many.) There were several elements which added to my overwhelming inability to adjust: Culture shock (the difference between the classroom of the sixties and the classroom of the eighties is phenomenal—I also have a sneaking suspicion that Utah schools, where I received my education and began my teaching career, differ in many ways from Georgia schools); my own change in life-style (there seemed to be little relationship between my belief that if the women I read about could handle a job and a family and look like movie stars, I could too, and the reality that I was already looking fat and frazzled and filling twenty-four hours a day *without* a job!); and my need for adulation (during my nineteen years of semi-retirement I had gone to graduate school, taught at two respected universities, written two books, and received a *lot* of positive strokes; as a struggling-to-keep-up low man on the totem pole I didn't find people anxious to join my fan club). The work was grueling, and I had little energy for building relationships. That year I gained an honest appreciation for the emotions Napoleon must have felt at Waterloo.

Compare my story with that of a twenty-nine-year-old secretary. Her burnout first manifested itself as marriage burnout. She became convinced that she wasn't important to her husband and suffered an enormous loss of self-esteem. "I felt he was too busy and too involved in 'his' world to really feel what was happening to me," she said. "I felt I wasn't good enough to be a part of his life. I looked for a way out, even considered divorce. I could not take care of my children—even they seemed to not need me." Then there was the forty-eight-year-old corporate treasurer who suffered parent burnout when she was rejected by a rebellious teenager. "I saw the beginnings of agoraphobia—it was a tremendous effort for me to leave my home; I just barely accomplished the routine household and parental tasks that had been simple for me at one time. I read books, played endless solitaire-type games, did crossword puzzles, constantly 'spun my wheels.' I was always tired and bored, and extremely dissatisfied with my life."

Intelligent, logical people can do stupid, illogical things when they become bogged down with the repeated lack of success that inevitably accompanies burnout. For the "clean living" Latter-day Saint, food is often the anesthetizing agent, although we all know that alcoholism and drug addiction are threats to the unhappy, hopeless individual even in our abstinent subculture. The theme of divorce ran through my research. Both men and women saw it as a possible way out, a change of scene, an escape from a life that had become uncomfortable, if not unbearable. Burning out youth and adults are also more susceptible to the temptation of sexual promiscuity and infidelity than are happy, living-in-the-here-and-now people.

Unless you are tuned in to the subtle symptoms of burnout it can sneak into your life and take over before you even stop to ask what hit you. You don't expect it because, remember, burnout victims are wonderful, self-sufficient people, and certainly not susceptible to human flaws like discouragement, disillusionment, or despair. But burnout is like excess weight and gum disease: It's easily managed if arrested early, but a tiger to cure when it gets out of hand. The symptoms may be mild at the beginning; watch for them.

If you used to manage well on six hours of sleep but now need ten, you may be going through a growth spurt *or* you may be burning out. If the ring of the telephone fills you with terror, you may be developing Pavlovsdogophobia (the fear of bells) or it may be the beginning of burnout. If you find yourself nitpicking or backbiting when you used to be easygoing and forgiving, ask yourself why. If you're a burnout beginner, you can stop the process early and become a better person by doing so. If your life is already a charred mess, you can save the pieces and start over. Even if you misdiagnose and discover your problems really are due to your age or your fears you haven't lost anything. The antidotes I suggest for burnout are all measures which will enrich your life and improve your outlook even if you're in pretty good shape already. You can't overdose on mental health if it's taken in its pure form.

Space

2

To the very young child, taking risks and making changes is a way of life. The toddler finds that the challenge of learning to walk far outweighs the fear of the pratfall. The nursery school child, pondering over the coordination toy, will repeatedly try, and fail, and try again, until he finally finds just the right space for the star-shaped puzzle piece. The happy, uninhibited spirit finds natural joy in discovery, in growth, and in progress, even when it involves a little pain.

As we grow older and experience our share of rebuffs and rejections something happens to the drive toward growth. At some stage of our lives, whether at fifteen or fifty, many of us make an unconscious decision that it is easier to live with our time-worn and comfortable hang-ups than to exert the effort it takes to get rid of them. While we may be able to reprogram a computer or rearrange a roomful of furniture, we assume a sort of paralysis when it comes to changing our innermost selves. Where living is concerned, old is not measured in birthdays. It is measured in terms of spiritual and intellectual energy.

As I muddled through the burned-out state, I was antiquity personified. I rationalized, blamed, criticized, and bellyached.

I was usually angry, sometimes openly and sometimes covertly, at someone or something: my coworkers, my boss, my family, ward members, and, of course, the all-purpose scapegoat, "The System." Most of the time I was able to maintain a mature and intelligent (albeit cynical) facade, but inside I could feel myself eroding. Still I continued to accuse everyone and everything that I saw as a stumbling block. It wasn't until I had exhausted all other resources and the pain became unbearable that I was willing to admit that the responsibility (it's more healthy not to think of it as fault, or guilt) might be mine.

Most of us do tend to blame burnout on external conditions. Of the people I questioned for this chapter, 16 percent said their burnout was due to their having too much to do. Eight percent blamed a disinteresting job, while another 8 percent named ways in which other people had contributed to their burned-out state (a child who had become involved with drugs, a husband who would not become interested in the Church, having to be around others who were not uplifting, indifference or lack of positive feedback from husband, a manipulative employer, and, from a teacher, indifferent students). Six percent pointed to a lack of appreciation from others, and 5 percent named the pressure to achieve, either exerted by others or by themselves.[1] Other reasons given were as follows:

4 Percent of Responses

Dislike for my job
Too much pressure (this group did not specify pressure to achieve so I took this response to mean pressure to meet deadlines, juggle time, etc.)

2 Percent of Responses

Rejection by others
Lack of measurable progress

---

1. Many respondents named more than one factor which contributed to burnout in their lives. All responses were assigned equal weight.

Space   *15*

Not enough living space
Financial problems
Spending too much time on a particular job
Dissatisfaction with self
The inability to say no
Losing control of specific situations
A job which inhibits creativity or free agency
A husband who travels or works long hours
No help

1 Percent of Responses

A limited scope of interest
Too much repetition and routine (in marriage)
Being hurt (emotionally) in a church job
Being taken advantage of
A lack of perspective
The fear of failure
Self-centeredness
No time for self
Lack of communication in marriage
Poor sex life
Staying too long in one place (job)
No way out
Going too fast
Physical problems
Being treated like a child
Moving
Sick of school
Specific family problems
Too much company (house guests)
Frustration with specific conditions

Eighty-five percent of the reasons given for burnout had to
do with external causes, leaving 15 percent which mentioned
causes generated from within. Interestingly, of the eight respondents who said no, they had never suffered burnout,
those few who chose to share their ideas concerning why they
had remained unaffected all centered on what they had done

as opposed to what had happened to them. One said that she had learned through experience to withdraw early from potential overcommitments. Another said: "When I start feeling overwhelmed I put up my feet and read a book or do a crossword puzzle, learn a new piece on the piano, or visit a friend. . . . I think my immunity to burnout is because of my congenital laziness." Then she went on to observe, "When we are going forward, do we get sick of it?"

By comparing the two types of responses, self- and outside-directed, I certainly don't mean to appear judgmental toward those of us who blame outside pressures. I wish to show, rather, that this is the natural thing to do. Still, it becomes increasingly clear to me that, natural or not, it is not the action-oriented thing to do. As I learned from my years of anger and frustration, when the need to be free from pain becomes greater than the need to place blame, there is only one important question: *What can I do to change things?*

It's true that overcommitment, boring work, and people who make our lives difficult *can* contribute to burnout. So can outside pressures, rejection, and a lack of space, both physical and emotional. While some of us can make some meaningful changes in these areas (learn to say no, get a better job, and associate with more uplifting friends) not all of us can all of the time. To the single working parent there's more to simplifying life than just refusing to chair the P.T.A. carnival. If the job you've got is the best you can get, making a change may be out of the question. If your downgrading associates happen to be your husband and children, then what? The often-quoted prayer, "God, grant me the serenity to accept the things I cannot change, courage to change the things I can, and wisdom to know the difference," implies that while some things can and should be changed, others must be accepted, at least for a time. Knowing that not all of our external circumstances are negotiable, I'd like to suggest some reasons for burnout that can be controlled from the inside.

Dr. Dean Black, Director of the Georgia Agency of LDS Social Services, believes that burnout is a major cause of distress for LDS individuals and families. He speaks both as a psychologist and as a bishop when he proposes that the princi-

Space   *17*

pal cause of burnout is a lack of balance in one's life. Dr.
Herbert J. Freudenberger, author of *Burn Out: How to Beat
the High Cost of Success,*[2] suggests a number of other reasons
that people suffer burnout. First, many of us approach a job or
an opportunity with expectations which are out of line with
reality. We burn out when we discover that the rewards of the
job, activity, marriage, or whatever, are not commensurate
with our expectations. Second, burnout can occur when we
are guided by a driving force, rather than a rational plan; in
other words, when we are driven rather than being in the
driver's seat. The belief that we can't make a difference can
also cause burnout, as can the practice of allowing ourselves to
be guided from without rather than from within. Finally,
burnout can be age-related, especially in people beginning to
approach middle age.

In *The Road Less Traveled* Dr. M. Scott Peck suggests that
the symptoms of depression and mental illness occur in order
to warn people that "they have taken the wrong path, that
their spirits are not growing and are in grave jeopardy."[3] In
other words, something has been amiss in our lives long before
the symptoms of depression, burnout, nervous breakdown, or
whatever, show up. Dr. Peck ventures further that the un-
pleasant symptoms are manifestations of grace, with the purpose of nurturing our spiritual growth. Looking at it this way I
feel compelled to make my knowledge that something is wrong
work for me.

This insight helps me to better understand my own
burnout cycle. While I didn't feel any serious ill effects until the
back-to-work episode, I can look back and see decisions I
made which led up to the inevitable job burnout.

About ten years previous to the time I write this, things
seemed to be going so well with me that I thought translation
was just around the corner. I was on a spiritual high to end all
spiritual highs. I had been called to the position of spiritual

_____

2. Dr. Herbert J. Freudenberger, Ph.D., with Geraldine Richelson, *Burn Out:
How to Beat the High Cost of Success* (New York: Doubleday and Company, 1980).

3. M. Scott Peck, M.D., *The Road Less Traveled* (New York: Simon and
Schuster, 1978).

living teacher in Relief Society and had been charged with the spiritual welfare of every woman in the ward. At the same time, in the setting-apart blessing I had been admonished (more like commanded) to fast before each lesson. This was when Relief Society was on a weekday, and I have never been a willing faster, but I accepted the challenge. (I was a little afraid not to!) The calling worked for me, and I worked for it, and I developed a closeness with the women in that ward that I've never experienced before or since. Spirituality permeated my life. I looked good. I felt good. My kids were happy. My house was clean. Everything jelled.

I lived under these utopian conditions for about a year, and then my husband accepted a job in another city. I felt good about the move. I like new challenges and new adventures, but I had conflicting thoughts about where I personally would be going. First, I knew I had something special and I didn't want to lose it, and I knew it was in jeopardy. A move always meant new adjustments, and there was a summer full of travel and visiting ahead. It would be easy, I knew, to slip back into my old and mundane self. And second, for some insane reason, I had the wild idea that since I had demonstrated (maybe received) a gift for working with women, I would immediately be made Relief Society president in my new ward. Why anyone would covet the job of Relief Society president is now beyond me, but in the far recesses of my mind I did then.

I arrived in my new ward and discovered that the Relief Society president was alive and well and quite stable. I was immediately called to be a counselor in the Primary. Please understand, this is nothing against the beautiful, sweet young spirits who hungered and thirsted after knowledge, but after a lifetime of teaching and mothering I admit to some disappointment at this call. I was shattered later when they sustained my best friend as a Relief Society teacher.

Still, the opportunities for service in that ward were phenomenal. There were always babies to sit with, dishes to be packed, houses to be cleaned, weddings to be catered, and nurseries to be manned. Just about the time I decided I wanted to be a writer they asked me to be the person in my ward in charge of tickets for the Washington Temple tours. Every day

Space 19

I'd kiss my kindergartner good-bye, sit down at the typewriter for a few hours of uninterrupted concentration, and the phone would start ringing. Could I make twenty thousand sandwiches for the entire state of New York, who would be coming for the temple dedication? How many people could I house? But first, clean the tile and grout in the new stake center . . .

Having just participated in the opening of the Atlanta Temple and seeing how very thrilled our members are for the *slightest* opportunity to serve I'm appalled at the bogged-down feeling I experienced in connection with the opening of the Washington Temple. There I was, in the midst of a historical and potentially very spiritual event, and I was complaining. (Check the list of burnout causes. I had allowed myself to be guided from without rather than from within. Instead of pacing myself and finding joy in service, I said yes grudgingly until I had to say no. I was experiencing a moderate case of church job burnout.)

I believe that many of us make the mistake of being guided from without in church work. We confuse what other people expect of us with what the Lord wants from us. The person who is driven from without says yes automatically, sometimes under the assumption that it is a sin to say no. However, because the person making the request has little knowledge (and sometimes, let's face it, little concern) regarding the individual status of the requestee, requests for help are sometimes ill-timed and unreasonable. At the same time, the requestee must take care not to confuse "what I want to do" with "what is best for me."

The person who is most effectively guided from within develops the habit of conducting a quick conference with the Spirit before answering a request. My fuse would have burned much longer if, for example, when I received the twelfth request for help in a week, I had learned to stop and think, *Let's see. It doesn't look like this is an urgent cry for help; no one's physical or mental health depends completely on my participation in this project. My laundry room is piled high and my kids can't get dressed this morning unless I make a dent in the dirty clothes. I think my family needs a little compassionate service today!* Having arrived at this conclusion through common sense I would then have asked for spiritual affirmation. If the prompting said, "You're right, stay home and put your own house in order," I could then spend the day washing my own clothes with a clear conscience. If it said, "This *is* urgent, and if you don't do it no one will; I'll help you with your housework later," then I'd render the service knowing that I was in the right place at the right time.

The person who is guided from within has several advantages. First, she seldom has trouble establishing priorities; second, by relying on the Spirit for direction she is also in a position to expect, and receive, extra heavenly help; and third, by receiving affirmation that she is doing the Lord's work she is less likely to become angry with other people for attempting to manipulate her or control her life.

It's been said that many of us live out our lives in quiet desperation. I also believe that many of us muddle through carrying large burdens of passive aggression. We go through life being all things to all people, sometimes seething underneath because we feel we're not appreciated, we're taken advantage of, or we've lost control of our lives (and what a frustrating feeling *that* is!). As I gain more insight into the principle of service I come closer and closer to understanding the meaning of 1 Corinthians 13:3, "And though I bestow all my goods to feed the poor, and though I give my body to be burned, and have not charity, it profiteth me nothing." It doesn't say it profiteth *the poor* nothing, but it profiteth *me* nothing; in fact, it may work to my detriment if I give grudgingly. I'm moving away from the concept of the Great Scorekeeper in the Sky and beginning to understand that good or bad is measured in terms of what it does to my insides. If rendering service gives me a warm, spiritual feeling then it's done me some good. If it makes me feel ill-used and taken advantage of I have still contributed a service—you can't take that away—but the angry feelings inside are certainly no good to me!

A woman I'll call Alyce attributes her church job burnout to working with a leader who was never quite satisfied:

"I remember burning out relatively quickly after working on the stake Relief Society board because my leader expected,

Space   *21*

and subtly demanded, 'big deals' one right after the other. For instance, I would prepare for a leadership meeting, and this lady wanted it 'nice' like you've never seen 'nice.' I would frantically write, prepare handouts, make posters and charts, decorate the room, color coordinate the refreshments and my outfit, and give a marvelous leadership meeting on Saturday. Then on Sunday morning, when I wanted to *forget* that I'd ever heard the words *Relief Society*, she'd call a board meeting and pass out an assignment to conduct a seminar that next week, etc., etc. No breathing room and no time to regroup between 'big deals.' "

Being guided from without rather than within can also be a contributing factor in marriage burnout. Sometimes we willingly submit ourselves to a condition of other-directedness when we mistakenly believe that we can only live the patriarchal order when we leave our individuality at the altar. One marriage burnout victim attributed her sense of frustration to "being forty and still being treated like a child by my husband —as though he had to discipline me, teach me, give me an allowance."

For most of us, the most challenging task associated with marriage has to do with being able to be "one" with another and yet remain an integrated individual. I was impressed by a sorority bumper sticker I saw which read "United but Unique." Couldn't that phrase describe a happily married couple?

Great bolts of insight hit me at the strangest times. Several years ago we had taken our children to King's Dominion, a large amusement park in Virginia. Since my twentieth birthday I have become green and queasy at the very thought of roller coasters and sky rides, so most of my time at parks is spent people-watching while my children ride. I noticed a woman, obviously from a middle eastern country, and my thoughts went back ten, no, it must have been nearly twenty years. I was sitting in "Dorm Council" in Lucy Mack Smith Hall at BYU. We'd tried and sentenced a number of penitent girls who had missed the 1:00 A.M. curfew. "I lost my watch." "We ran out of gas." "We couldn't find the submarine races." All logical and believable excuses. Our next offender was a young woman from Iran. In her broken English she gave what, to her, was a perfectly acceptable reason for breaking what must certainly, she thought, have been an arbitrary rule. "In my country, we do what the man says. (With awe:) If he says it's time to go, we go. If he says stay, we stay."

Member of the jury: "But you knew dorm hours ended at one o'clock. Couldn't you have reminded him?"

Offender (shocked): "Oh, no! That would have been disrespectful!"

Sitting outside the tilt-a-whirl and looking at the woman in the sari, I was hit with the irony of it all. As young women many of us learn to value independence and self-direction. Then we get married and some of us get the impression that we're supposed to go from self-sufficient to submissive overnight. Often we lose something in the translation.

The husband who doesn't understand the meaning of *stewardship* or who misinterprets the word *power* as it relates to his priesthood can contribute to feelings of frustration in his bewildered wife. The woman who "plays the role" of the submissive wife only to stifle her own spiritual qualities will one day have to deal with suppressed anger, low self-esteem, and perhaps a lack of direction. While some women seem to be innately adaptable and have no problem making the transition from independent individual to happy helpmeet, others flounder. To them, learning to be genuine, authentic selves who foster the growth of other genuine, authentic selves through love and joy is a life's work. It is quite possible that they will experience an episode of burnout in the process.

Some employees become immobilized when they are over-administered and given no leeway for individuality and creativity. Kids may become discouraged when they are over-parented and constantly nagged, advised, and checked up on. All of us need space. We all need a sense of autonomy. Some of us need to learn to give room for growth. Others need to learn to take it.

We Are Driven 3

There is a professor at the university I attend whom I dearly love except for one thing. He is always analyzing me. I could tolerate this except for one thing. He is usually right.

For instance, the last class I took from him was conducted at a high school in Snellville. Now, Snellville's okay, but you can hardly get there from where I work. It's an hour-long drive if traffic isn't backed up, but the trouble is, you never know. Construction or an accident on the freeway (commonplace occurrences) can draw it out to at least an hour and a half. And the route from Smyrna (where I teach) to Snellville isn't a big item on the sky-copter traffic report.

I admit now that the trip from my school to my class takes an hour or more, but, strangely, during the entire ten weeks that my class was in session I thought of it as a forty-five-minute drive. The class started at 4:00, and inevitably, whether I was in a mad rush or enjoying a leisurely afternoon, I left at 3:15. I was continually shocked and panic stricken when the radio announcer declared "4:00!" and I was still on the freeway.

One afternoon my professor expounded on passive aggression. "One of the most common ways of expressing passive aggression," he said, "is by being late." He went on to describe my behavior, and I was both curious and furious. Certainly not in my case! What reason did I have to express anger, either actively or passively? It was just a class, and I had no reason to dislike either the professor or any of the other students. The case study had nothing to do with me, I decided.

Somewhat defensively I related the incident to a complete stranger in the restroom during the break. "Well," she responded, "I don't know about you, but it certainly could be *my* reason!" The bell rang, and I could only guess what she was thinking.

On the way home I thought about the class. True, I felt no animosity toward the professor or the other students, but I did resent having to take that class. It was a prerequisite for a practicum, which I dreaded. It was a class I'd taken years ago, and I'd had to repeat it because of the undeniable evolution of the subject matter. I even resented taking education classes. With my current interests, wouldn't I be better off in psychology or English? The more I thought, the more agitated I became. Of course I was angry! Why shouldn't I be?

When I became honest with myself I realized that I'd had a history of tardiness. Was I angry with the whole human race? I never wanted to be early for a meeting. Why should I be early and waste my time waiting for others? Better far that they should wait for me! I thought about my job. I was never late enough to get in trouble, just late enough to satisfy my compulsion. I nearly always heard the 7:30 bell as I stepped from my car into the parking lot.

Being places on time is not an issue here. Neither is passive aggression. I expose my problem with punctuality in order to acquaint you with compulsion. Compulsion: "An irresistible inner force compelling the performance of an act without, or even against, the will of the individual performing it."[1] I never intended to be late. Conversely, I think of myself as dependable, efficient, and considerate. By continuing to fool myself

---

1. James Drever, *The Penguin Dictionary of Psychology* (New York: Penguin Books, 1952).

into thinking the drive to Snellville was forty-five minutes, I allowed my compulsive lateness to control me. Rather than rationally deciding that if I was late when I left at 3:15 I might want to try leaving at 3:00, I rigidly maintained that if I left earlier I might be *too* early and thus waste my time. I was compelled to be late.

By admitting that I have compulsions, I am by no means admitting that I am a compulsive person. Although the diagnostician may need to use labels from time to time, we don't. There is no shame in admitting, especially to ourselves, that we have certain neurotic tendencies—everyone does. Yours may be different from mine, but we all have them. Some people have a hard time making decisions. Some have irrational fears. Some are bothered by feelings of inadequacy, guilt, or self-blame. When we are oversensitive, continually angry, resentful, or defensive we are exhibiting neurotic tendencies, just as we are when we feel we have to please everyone. Spinning your wheels (when the hurrieder you go the behinder you get), thinking illogically, being too shy for your own comfort, exhibiting psychosomatic symptoms, being self-centered—I could go on, but I won't. No one is completely sane, so why should any of us claim to be?

Behaving compulsively is just one of the things we do to show we're still human and not quite ready for the Meritorious Medal for Marvelous Mental Health, which is tantamount to being in a state of translatability. Our compulsions may inconvenience or embarrass us. While we *can* get rid of them, at present they're as much a part of our personalities as the way we talk and the way we walk.

Not everyone can have every compulsion. Some are mutually exclusive. Some people are compulsively neat, others are compulsively sloppy. Some are compulsive eaters, others compulsive starvers. You can be compulsively late or compulsively punctual. You can be a compulsive achiever or a compulsive nonachiever. Logically, some compulsions are more convenient than others.

My compulsions are all inconvenient. Not only am I compulsively late; I also have a weird compulsion to always leave my kitchen just a *little* bit cluttered. I often eat compulsively and talk compulsively. My compulsions have no redeeming features.

Some people, on the other hand, have convenient compulsions. Convenient in the sense that they look good from the outside, *not* that they make them feel particularly good. They don't. A woman with a compulsion for neatness and cleanliness will probably get a lot of strokes from envious friends and appreciative real estate agents. The compulsively punctual person is appreciated by everyone, with the possible exception of the compulsively late hostess. The compulsive achiever receives accolades from parents, teachers, and employers. Hopefully, anyway, because he needs them. Desperately.

It's this compulsive achiever we talk about when we say that burnout can occur when we are guided from a driving force rather than a rational plan. Here I am not talking about being guided from *without,* as I did in chapter 2. When we are guided from without, there is another person involved. When we are guided by a driving force, that force is inside us. It is us, but it is not the rational thinking part of us. Neither is it the spiritual part of us, because the driving force we talk about here is potentially destructive, and a spiritual force is of necessity constructive. We *can* be compelled by the Spirit, and we'll discuss that possibility later.

The variable that sets the compulsive achiever apart from anyone else who has ever achieved is motivation. There are many completely healthy reasons for achieving. You don't have to be compulsive to know the thrill of accomplishment. Creativity and excellence are their own rewards. We can achieve great things for practical reasons—money, for example. It's right to give an honest day's work for a day's wages, and we are even admonished to go the extra mile. Your basic, no-hang-ups achiever achieves because it feels good and/or it's profitable. Or simply because it's right.

The compulsive achiever, on the other hand, achieves great things because he's afraid not to. He believes, way down inside, that if he doesn't accomplish great feats, he will have to admit that he's inadequate, unworthy, or unacceptable. He is terrified of failure, having never learned that even loveable and capable folks botch it up sometimes. He must constantly prove his right to exist, and he does this through his fantastic accomplishments.

Although I must admit to knowing some people who fit the profile of the Compulsive Achiever pretty neatly, as in other pigeonholes, most of us don't fit completely. Some of us, like me, phase in and out of the list of characteristics. I am more driven, for example, than is my serene and easygoing friend Suzanne, but less driven than another friend, Ridley Bigelow. As you read, don't be defensive and think *What's wrong with that?* and don't be embarrassed, thinking *Who, me?* While people who have a great many of the characteristics I am about to describe often have (or *give*) problems, some don't. If you fit the profile perfectly and you're happy and your family is happy, don't worry about it! If you're driven, and you enjoy being driven, don't relax and reduce your monthly income on my account! You may be one of the favored few who can make your compulsion work for you, and will go down in the annals of Wall Street history, or you may find, in five or ten years, that you do feel a need to regroup. If you don't fit the profile of the compulsive achiever but you know someone who does, don't, whatever you do, run to that person and shout "Hey, this is you!" You'll only make them more compulsive.

There is a fine line separating the compulsive achiever from the compulsive worker. Nearly all compulsive achievers are compulsive workers, but not all compulsive workers are achievers. Some workers go about a task so compulsively that they waste time. They are the group that people refer to when they say, "They work hard, but they don't work smart." Others are so tied up in knots with anxiety that while they feel a desperate need to achieve, they can't accomplish anything. Just as the compulsive eater has a lot in common with the anorexic, the inner workings of the overachiever (if there is such a thing) and the underachiever are very similar.

Basically, compulsive workers/achievers share these characteristics: They work extremely hard, and put in more than the required amount of time on the project at hand. While some compulsive achievers dedicate their lives to their jobs, others lend their intense zeal to a variety of causes: Church work, community service, sports, the arts, even hobbies. A compulsive stamp collector won't stop until he's put together the most complete stamp collection in the county (the state? . . . the nation? . . .).

People who are driven from within are described as being rigid in their thinking, focused in their attention, and somewhat ritualistic.[2] Because of these traits perspective is often a problem. It's quite possible that the executive who is unable to unwind long enough to play ball with his anxious but awkward preschooler or the salesman who repeatedly works late on his wedding anniversary are so centered on their need for achievement that it is impossible for them to see the important necessities on the periphery. The mother who can't miss a day of work to stay with a sick child is an example of an extreme focus on work, as is, on the other hand, the ritualistic homemaker who won't ever do compassionate service on a Monday, because it's wash day. The driven find it painful, if not impossible, to shift priorities.

Men and women who are driven are fiercely competitive, with themselves as well as with others. They are extremely active, and they have an amazing ability to suppress feelings which might interfere with the reaching of their goals. People who are driven from within have a great need to exercise control, not only over their work, but over their environment as a whole. They abhor (I don't mean just a healthy *dislike*) failure, boredom, and laziness.

Far be it from me to determine where compulsivity leaves off and greatness begins. It is my personal belief that while some of the great successes of our time were/are driven by a desperate need to succeed, others have transcended this inner drive and get their amazing energy from a more dependable source. One way to determine the source of power is that the person who is self-directed can enjoy his successes and accept his failures, whereas to the "driven" individual nothing is ever enough. He never feels successful; he always needs more. The harder the compulsive achiever works for approval, the more

---

2. David Shapiro, *Neurotic Styles* (New York: Basic Books, Inc., 1965).

elusive that approval becomes. As an attractive, talented, and efficient young woman observed, "I burned out from being 'wonderful' for too long to too many people, and finding people expected from me rather than looking at me and appreciating me." In an extensive and enlightening study of the workaholic, Marilyn Machlowitz shares a classic illustration of the "driven" mentality as she quotes a renowned scientist: "My philosophy has always been that second best is the loser."[3]

Again, if you must have compulsions, the compulsion to achieve is a most convenient one. Compulsive achievers get more money, more positive strokes, and more press than do their more tranquil, easy-to-please peers. Some even claim they are happier. If an idle mind is the devil's playground, what better way to help stamp out sin than perpetual motion?

Frankly, the driven individual probably suffers less from his compulsive state than do those around him. His only potential problem is that his power is not necessarily unlimited. The energy that drives the compulsive achiever does not spring from a deep, unexpendable source; it is manufactured and forced. The achiever is, then, subject not only to burnout, but to stress-related ailments (stroke, heart attack, ulcers . . .) as well. While the "Driven" *are* usually happy as long as they continue to achieve and obtain recognition, woe unto them when disaster strikes, either in the form of a job they can't handle, an illness or accident that forces them to slow down, or a reduction in staff which renders them suddenly unemployed. The emotional high of the compulsive achiever is conditional.

It is often the families and those working under the compulsive achiever who suffer most from the driving force. "The Driven" are often most inconvenient spouses. As an over-the-counter tranquilizer commercial once observed, "Behind every successful man there's a — (pregnant pause) — *nervous wreck.*" Compulsive achievers don't like to be bothered with everyday household tasks and errands, yet they want their homes to run as smoothly as their offices. They often look on their families

---

3. Marilyn Machlowitz, *Workaholics: Living with Them, Working with Them* (New York: Mentor, 1980), p. 127.

as extensions of themselves, and expect their wives (I wanted to make this completely nonsexist and put "mates," but let's face it, in our subculture the successful business achiever is still primarily, although not solely, the husband) and kids to be well-dressed, accomplished, and exemplary. As I noted earlier, the compulsive achiever has a strong need to control his environment, and he or she may not be able to delineate between their "environment" and the lives of others. To complicate matters even further, compulsive achievers have a difficult time forming close relationships. We'll discuss in later chapters ways to deal with family and work problems associated with compulsive achievers.

When I finally realized what havoc my own compulsions were wreaking in my life, I began to think of *compulsion* as a dirty word, one to be avoided at all costs. I became conscious of not only an increasing number of compulsive behaviors in myself, but, naturally, an inordinate number of compulsive behaviors in my fellows! Then I started hearing the word *compelled* being tossed around in my one refuge from the weird and crazy world, in *church!* In one fast meeting alone I heard several people say they felt "compelled" to bear their testimonies. Others told about times they had felt compelled to do something they hadn't wanted to do, like stop smoking and join the Church. Then, to top it all off, we had the Relief Society lesson about the lady who felt compelled to go inside to see whether she'd turned off the iron.

Well, that almost did it! To refresh your memories, the lesson was on personal revelation, and one of the illustrations told about a woman who had, as many of us do, packed for a trip in a frenzy. Finally, with toothbrushes packed and dishes washed, she sat with her family in the car preparing for take-off. As they drove out of the driveway she calmly asked her husband to stop. She'd had a hunch about the iron she'd been using. While the family waited she went inside to make sure she'd pulled out the plug. She hadn't, and the lesson went on to point out that she'd been guided to go back and unplug the iron; otherwise a fire would have undoubtedly started and devastated her house while the family was on their trip.

To all the non-obsessive-compulsive sisters in the audience, that was a faith-promoting story. All the obsessive-compulsive ones, and some on the borderline, thought it was funny. We *always* went back in the house after it was locked up to check the iron, the oven, the curling iron—some of us two or three times! To us, it would be a miracle if we ever got out of the driveway *without* going back to check the iron! I can remember driving to work thinking "I did." "I didn't." "Did I?" "I *think* so . . ." and trying to visualize the exact moment I disconnected the plug of my cheap and potentially explosive curling iron. Many times. My kids are accustomed to being awakened by the ring of the telephone and an anxious voice ordering, "I need you to do a favor for me. Go into my bathroom and look . . ." Before I'd even finish, a sleepy voice would always answer, "Sure, Mom. We'll check your curling iron."

They got me, though, last April Fools' Day. The same sleepy voice answered the phone, but the cast had been alerted. When the phone rang, they'd taken their posts—one pressing the button of the smoke alarm, the other far enough from the upstairs extension to make it sound natural, shouting "Fire! Fire!" The sleepy voice said: "No problem, Mom. Your curling iron is fine. You *did* leave the broiler oven on full blast, though, with what seems to have been a cube of butter melting inside. Can't talk too long, I've got to call the fire department. But, Mom, can we get the new platinum-colored appliances when we redo the kitchen?"

When I had to face the fact that not all compulsions were crippling I started trying to compartmentalize compulsions. Which ones were spiritually based? Which ones were self-doubt based? When was it compulsive to go back and check the curling iron and when was it inspiration? I formed the subject of my next women's conference address in my mind: "Can we have excellence without compulsiveness?" So much of the Church is achievement oriented, but every now and then we hear something about peace and tranquility. The relentlessly driven individuals I knew were anything but serene.

I'm still finding answers. For me it has to be a spiritual process; the intellectual answers are elusive. I'm discovering that yes, there are spiritual compulsions, and they can be a very positive force. I'm also learning that, in situations like the great curling iron turnoff, the spiritual compulsion can't always be distinguished from the neurotic compulsion. That is a very good reason for me to get rid of my neurotic compulsions, so I'll be free to recognize a spiritual prompting when I feel one. I can almost always determine the source of a compulsion *after* I've acted on it. The neurotic compulsion is linked to a feeling of tension, of striving, of "now what?" The spiritual compulsion brings peace and excitement. And *energy*.

It's the energy that I'm after, that makes it worth my while to completely revamp my life-style. I've come to the point where I've done about all I can do on my own, and I'm going to have to have some extra help if I'm going to be able to do all the things I have to do and some of the things I want to do without going bonkers; if I'm to stretch that twenty-four-hours-a-day to the maximum. I've come to understand the meaning of John 15:5, "without me ye can do nothing." I want to be connected to that never-ending fountain of life. But I can't connect with it as long as my life is cluttered with my own compulsive wants and needs, as long as I conduct my rigid life with tunnel vision. If I'm going to lengthen my stride I'm going to have to learn an entirely new way of walking.

Stride lengthening is a case in point. I'll never forget the day I first heard the admonition. It had been one of those weeks, and by Saturday morning I felt that I'd been put through a wringer. I'd been faced with the stereotypic Saturday decision: Do I go to stake leadership meeting or to my son's football game? At the last minute that problem was solved—the game was rained out. I'd been up at 5:00 washing and cleaning and trying to make up for the week I'd spent running in circles: There'd been casseroles to deliver, work at the cannery, a party for my daughter's class at school, and never enough time. My Primary job seemed to grow more demanding with each day, and we'd had out-of-town house-guests recently. By 9:00 A.M. I had thrown myself together and was headed for my 10:00 meeting. I figured I'd be on time if I hit the green lights just right. But the rain which had enabled me to attend the meeting hadn't worked only for my convenience. The road was flooded, and the trip to the stake center was complicated by detours and traffic jams. Wet and exhausted I took my place in the chapel after the opening prayer and song. The stake Primary president was giving an inspirational talk to buoy us up. We still needed to improve, she told us; now was no time for resting on laurels. Exhausted and bedraggled I heard the phrase that was yet to become a slogan: Lengthen Your Stride.

Some of our latter-day shibboleths, like Mend Your Fences and Brighten Your Understanding had appealed to me as exciting and readily acceptable. But somehow, sloshing as I was that day in my soggy sandals, and feeling as I did that no matter how fast I ran I could never catch up, I resented that reminder. *If my present speed isn't acceptable*, I kept thinking, *I don't know what is. I'm giving it all I've got.*

I contended with that counsel for years, then more or less managed to forget it, until one of my friends from our Church Social Services Agency called and invited me to speak at their annual conference. I accepted enthusiastically. What an opportunity! I was submerged in research for another book, *Don't Trip on Your Clouds of Glory*, and there were so many things I couldn't wait to share. Depression would be a great subject for a social services conference, or what about losing yourself in the work versus getting yourself lost in the shuffle? Automatically, I inquired whether there was a particular subject they'd like me to address. Well, since you asked, said my friend, the theme of the conference was Lengthen Your Stride. It would be great if I could talk about that.

My work was cut out for me. In a way, asking me to talk on that subject was like asking Billy Martin to expound on the joys of winning the coveted sportsmanship trophy. But I like a well-coordinated program, and I decided I'd adhere to the theme if it took a change of heart to do it. I gave up my books in favor of prayer and meditation, and in time for the meeting I received about thirty minutes worth of truth and light. As I prepared my speech I was able to see stride lengthening from a completely new perspective, to distinguish quality of life from quantity of work. The prophet was suggesting that I lengthen my stride, I discerned, *not* asking me to run more frantically.

This illustration came to me. What if you had an old used car and you decided you wanted to go in for drag racing? You could do one of two things. You could either feed it gas relentlessly and drive it until you completely wore it out, or you could do what we used to call "soup up the engine." If you used the original engine and held the pedal to the metal unmercifully it would probably give you a little extra speed, as long as it lasted, but the stress would eventually get to it and it would blow a gasket or something. (Is it obvious that I'm not an auto mechanic?) If, on the other hand, you decided to "soup it up," and you rebuilt the engine so there would be more power from within and less necessity to exert pressure and stress from the driver's seat, your car would probably go faster and last longer. By improving the source of power from within, you have a better chance of getting the results you want.

With the understanding that the key to stride lengthening was not more self-administered stress but more God-given power, I began to look at the areas of my own life that would profit from a complete overhaul. After some honest soul-searching I was able to coin some slogans of my own.

First, Shrink Your Stomach. This suggestion is not for everyone, only those of you who, like me, find that dragging around a few extra pounds robs you of a lot of energy. I figure that the twenty or thirty excess pounds I carry cost me at least two hours of what otherwise would be productive time during the day. Add that to the time I would save if I were able to walk through the kitchen without stopping at the refrigerator, and you've got a considerable amount of time. Of course, any improvements you can make on your body will help both your energy level and your spirituality. While the junkfood lover in me tries not to acknowledge this, it's true that nutrition makes a big difference. Just read the Word of Wisdom in its entirety sometime! And I'll guarantee that regular exercise will have a positive effect in all areas of your life.

Next, Forgive Your Enemies. Feelings of hatred, distrust, disdain, hostility, jealousy, and the urge for revenge play havoc with your insides and rob you of the serenity you need to order your life. When you get rid of those feelings it is possible for the Spirit to work in your behalf.

Closely related to the inability to forgive is the habit some of us have of judging others. Recently a friend and I were

We Are Driven

talking about someone and really getting into a tirade about all the things this person was doing to botch up her life. As we talked I felt an anxious feeling come into my stomach, almost like a poison creeping into my system. The thought occurred to me, *Wouldn't life be simple if we didn't feel that we had to judge other people?* and I was reminded of the scripture which says "for with what judgment ye judge, ye shall be judged" (Matthew 7:10). I suddenly felt a great sense of relief surge through me, as I realized that I didn't *have* to pass judgment on this person, and not only that, if I could just learn *not* to judge people, my own judgment day would be a piece of cake![4] Judging, like holding a grudge, takes a lot of energy.

My last suggestion is Get to Know Your Spirit. I mention this last because it is a lot easier to do this if you have conquered the first two. In fact, any law or commandment that you keep makes it a lot easier to follow this suggestion.

When we were in heaven we were, of course, spirit beings. We weren't hampered by physical needs and appetites. We knew who we were and had been taught what was best for us. We weren't perfected, because we hadn't had enough experience to be perfected, but we *were* spiritual.

Then we came to earth and were given a physical body. This body could go one of two ways. It could subject itself to the spirit within it or it could overwhelm this spirit. The people you know who seem to be living on a celestial plane much of the time are those who have chosen to subject the body to the spirit. Those who seem to be completely wicked and without redeeming features are those who have chosen to let their bodies overwhelm their spirits. Most of us vascillate between the two extremes.

It was a long time before I could see the advantages of letting my spirit rule my body. Somewhere I got the idea that the spiritual person was a sanctimonious, rigid person who didn't really have a lot of fun. This was fine for eternity, but it didn't fit my idea of what I wanted for myself during this life. I was almost afraid to put my life in God's hands because in the

---

4. After my recent preachment regarding nutrition, maybe "a bowl of sprouts" is a better figure of speech.

back of my mind I was sure that his idea of a good time was not the same as mine. I went about my life making my own decisions, always in keeping with what I knew about right and wrong and the Church's stand on things, but I was never able to let go of my life. I found as I carried out my do-it-yourself decisions that I experienced a growing sense of uneasiness. As I progressed along the path I had mapped out for myself I felt like the airline pilot whose voice came over the speaker and said: "I have some good news and some bad news. The bad news is that we're lost. I have no idea where we're headed. The good news is that we're making good time."

The uneasy feeling, together with the fact that I somehow wasn't getting to where I wanted to be, made me more and more uncomfortable. You might say miserable. I became depressed; I became lethargic. Talk about finding it hard to get out of bed in the morning! It finally got so bad that I thought of the old saying, "When all else fails, read the directions." But I didn't *read* the directions, I asked for them. I got down on my knees and said, in essence, "I give up. My way isn't working. Just let me know what I'm supposed to do, and I'll do it." Once I was desperate enough and prayed hard enough, I was ready to let go and be led. And some funny things happened when the answers started coming. I discovered that as I learned to rely on the Spirit more, I learned to rely on the approval of other people less. My spiritual self, I discovered, had self-esteem to spare. It was creative, funny, and a lot smarter than my physical self. I learned that I had underestimated my Heavenly Father's taste in entertainment. This thing they called joy was a real high! My spiritual self was nothing like the dull person I had feared she would be.

The more I learn about life, the more conscious I become of paradox. Now, years after I delivered the Lengthen Your Stride speech, I am amazed that I was able to verbalize these ideas then but I am still trying to actualize them now. Line upon line, precept on precept, I'm starting to understand what I said that night.

I couldn't, or wouldn't, change until my narrow and unproductive way of life became too painful. As my Father in Heaven saw that I was finally serious about wanting to

We Are Driven   37

change, the Spirit started working within me. *I felt compelled to get rid of my compulsions!* The way to do this was revealed —sometimes through an inner understanding, sometimes through sources I was led to: books, friends, speeches. Usually the two—outside sources and inside affirmation—worked together. I came to accept some rather inconvenient precepts. Relationships are more important than accomplishments. "No man is an island." Change what you can and forget what you can't. Learn to let go.

Will I ever get there? Probably not in this life, but at least I'll be headed in the right direction when I die. Of course I backslide. Every time I go on vacation or go back to school in the fall, or otherwise find myself in a new situation, I find myself reverting back to my old self-inflicted habits. But those moments when I am making an honest effort to let go of "the natural man" within me are full of joy and excitement. Hopefully when I have more of these memories on which to meditate the upward climb will become easier. I'm counting on it.

If I've got it figured right, my life is at least half over. I was baptized at eight, and it's taken me this long to learn that faith, repentance, and the gift of the Holy Ghost are really the answer to overcoming my harassing hang-ups. Am I the only one, I wonder, or is there a goodly number of Latter-day Saints who find themselves doing all the right things for the wrong reasons?

I'm reminded of an incident my husband related to me while he was in graduate school at a large university in the midwest. He had handed in what was apparently an outstanding research paper. His professor called him up after class and commented on it. After a few honest compliments the professor asked earnestly, "What is it about you Mormons? I have known many of you, and every Mormon I've met has been at the head of his class, top in his field, extremely competent, and, it almost seems, very competitive. Why?" He went on to give a couple of his own theories. Like the rental car company who tried harder because they were number two, we had to prove ourselves because we were a persecuted minority. We were instilled with a sense of pride and heritage. The Church stressed achievement. My husband and I discussed it afterward and decided it could be any of the above, or it could be something more.

"As for me and my house," achievements continue to be an important part of our lives. My goal is not to achieve less, certainly, but to refine my reasons for achieving so I might enjoy my accomplishments more. While it does make me proud to hear about the accomplishments of fellow Church members, I don't want to do well simply in order to prove something to someone. And while a sense of pride in one's heritage is an admirable quality, I don't want my children to achieve just to make me proud. I would like to be able to say: "I accomplish things because to do so makes me happy. There is a great sense of joy which accompanies a good job well done. Further, my ability to accomplish increases as I grow in spirituality. I have learned to connect with that source of energy and creativity which will never dry up or burn out."

I'm progressing. Last night I actually arrived at a meeting five minutes early. I fasted this fast day without obsessing over food. I cleaned my kitchen and it stayed that way for hours. But I've got to end this chapter now. I have to make sure I unplugged the curling iron.

What in the Dickens Is Wrong with Great Expectations? **4**

Every Christmas season at least one of the leading magazines carries an article about seasonal depression, addressing the fact that more people suffer feelings of dejection at Christmastime, the time of year which has long been associated with joy and happiness, than at any other season of the year. Each article will treat the question, "Why do people feel depressed at Christmas?" from a different frame of reference. Too much sugar. Money worries. Too much commercialism. Unrealistic expectations.

If I had to choose one that best accounted for *my* occasional holiday doldrums it would be the last. Expectation. Even as an adult I hold on to the hope that I will somehow recapture the Christmas magic I felt as a child. Each holiday season I wait for the intense emotions of anticipation and realization that once enchanted me. Reluctantly I realize that such extreme emotions are reserved for children. Even on good years, when I'm able to feel the "right" spirit—the one that comes from giving and sharing and creating and appreciating —I get a more subdued, peaceful feeling. The sleepless nights spent listening for reindeer hooves and the eventual amazement that Santa had visited our house without my hearing him, and had left the most exquisite doll imaginable, are gone forever. Compared to my early memories Christmas will always be a disappointment until I revise my expectations.

A close second to Christmas in terms of expectation versus realization is what many girls experience on Prom Night. Surely from the far reaches of your past you can dredge up a memory like this. You're sixteen, and you've known all along that underneath that sweet and studious spirit of yours is a real dynamite dazzler. Though you're not, by any means, the homecoming queen type, you're not all that bad, either, and you've heard it said that you've got a great personality. After weeks of fervent prayer your dream is realized. Some guy in your algebra class (not Mr. Muscle, but a nice looking guy in his own right) asks you to the prom. Your dismal life as a daydreamer is over. Cinderella, eat your heart out!

In the absence of a fairy godmother you beseech your father, who works, or your mother, who sews. You arrive at a compromise. They'll spend a few more dollars on a dress if you'll agree to show a little less skin. You finally find the right gown, one that transforms you from Average Alice to Radiant Rita. You stock up on Oxy-5 and swear off chocolate. During the next few weeks you could make honor society or flunk out of school. It wouldn't matter. Your efforts and your dreams are directed toward the dance.

Finally the night arrives, and you dress with just a few disappointments. Worst, the sickening realization that the shameless wretch who charged you ten dollars to pile your gorgeous hair on top of your head has made you look more like your mother than like the picture you cut out of *Vogue* magazine. Next-to-worst, the silent sinking in your heart when you see the soft pink roses your date has brought to offset your fiery crimson gown. And why did he bring a wrist corsage when there is plenty of fabric on your shoulders? *Obviously,* you think, *this kid has never met my father.*

You had visualized yourself as the most beautiful one there, or at least in the running, but reality rails. On a scale of 10, you are a 3⅓. Compared to Karen Brown, who *is* the homecoming queen type, you look tacky. Compared to Sherry Sheffield, the cheerleader type, you are too prim and reserved. Your date is about as outgoing and sought after as you are, so you spend the night alternately dancing and sitting, trying to make conversation. It's painful. And if that weren't humiliation enough, a look at yourself in the powder room at intermission reveals the worst. Dark perspiration marks under your arms. Red blotches on your neck from the lace in your dress and the anxiety of the evening. Gravity has played havoc with your upswept hairdo, and the plastered effect from the thick shield of hairspray gives it a bizarre effect. You'd give anything to be home with your friends in your jeans and sweatshirt, watching TV and sending out for pizza.

Another example of how unrealistic expectations can cause problems has to do with the family who joins the Church and moves to Utah. They expect a gathering place of the Saints, with a capital S, and they find just another community, with some saints and some sinners, and what's worse, some of the sinners are found among the Saints! The expectation is that all Mormons live their religion to the letter, and even beyond. The reality is that Latter-day Saints, like any other group, form a normal curve. They run the gamut from dedicated, honest, and generous at one extreme to bitter, slothful, and despicable at the other, with a lot of well-intentioned but imperfect mortals clustered around the mean. The convert who finds himself in a neighborhood with a hypocritical high priest next door and an angry apostate across the street usually finds himself bitterly disappointed and disillusioned. Unless he can realistically reassess his expectations and realize that it's making the gospel work in his own life that matters, he is opening himself to alienation and possible apostasy.

Next to Christmas, the biggest discrepancy between expectation and reality in my own life is Sunday. I expect Sunday to be a day of rest. I'm just beginning to realize that the reason Sunday is really a day of rest for some people is that they work all week to make their day of rest happen. My Sundays were restful and rejuvenating until I had kids. Then the battle began. Not the battle between me and my kids, the battle between me and the day. My body refuses to function on Sunday. No matter that people have to be fed and clothed and cleaned up after, *I* am supposed to *rest*. Therefore, I resent every bit of work I have to do. Sunday is a trial for me. Not only do I not get to rest, but I work myself into a frenzy worrying about it!

Christmas, Prom Night, our preconceived notions of "Zion," the Sunday doldrums—whatever. Unrealistic expectations in any area of our lives can cause despair. Sometimes the expectations don't even have to be unrealistic to cause trouble. We can make ourselves unhappy simply by insisting that we should have what we want when we want it. When we go into a job or a relationship with inflexible preconceived notions of what we expect to gain from the experience, we set ourselves up for potential disappointment. Sometimes our expectations are realized and we go on our various merry ways, believing that life will always fill our prescriptions to the letter. But occasionally they're not, and we experience bewilderment and the beginnings of bitterness. Isn't it *right* to want our job, our marriage, our family, our presidency, to be the Very Best? Aren't we accepting mediocrity when we settle for a job, a mate, or a first counselor that doesn't quite meet our standard of excellence?

Now we're getting down to the nitty gritty of fine lines and paradoxes, where rigid thinking must give way to an openness to inspiration. Yes, it's good to expect the best—of ourselves, of others, of our lives. But our expectations serve us best when they are tempered with flexibility. Perhaps in this context *expectation* is the wrong word. The trouble comes when we *demand* that our expectations are met, and we become immobilized when they're not. Expectations are great when they are expressed in the form of high hopes, hard work, or hanging on, and our own expectations play an important role in our level of achievement. But when unrealized hopes lead you to a feeling of despair, anger, or disillusionment, it's time to examine your expectations.

Burnout occurs when a person finds himself in a situation (a job or a relationship, for instance) in which the rewards are not commensurate with the expectation. I'll borrow from my experience with teacher burnout to provide an example.

In a way, my early teaching experience set me up for my problem. An enthusiastic new college graduate, I approached

What in the Dickens Is Wrong with Great Expectations? 43

my first teaching job with all the idealism one might expect in a young, high achieving crusader. I expected to make a difference. I expected people to love me. I expected to design the curriculum to end all curricula, to decorate the ultimate gorgeous learning environment. It may sound a little sickening to you nonidealists, but that was what I wanted, and that was about what I got. The world was ready for me. I was ready for it. Conditions in my school jibed perfectly with conditions in my heart. Also, I was relatively free to pursue my goals. I was newly married, had a husband who studied a lot, and lived in a tiny, undemanding apartment. If I wanted to stay until dark preparing a unit of study, I could. Once I even got locked in the school building! My first job lived up to my expectations, and I lived up to my expectations of myself. If there had been a Camelot, Utah, I would have applied to teach there.

Years later, when I left my four-bedroom house and three kids to take up where I left off, I intended to do just that. What I didn't know was that during the fifteen or so years that I was home taking care of my children, the world had conspired against me. They'd changed the rules. "Teach the whole child" had given way to "Get them to pass the test." My autonomy had been rescinded. The paperwork had multiplied. Plus, I'd lost my youth and I was now one of the multitude of middle-aged, no longer the "cute young teacher with all the energy."

I felt that I'd been betrayed. Betrayed by my superiors, who seemed to care more that I'd used more than my share of ditto paper than that I'd opened someone's mind. Betrayed by "the system," which seemed to have no use for the qualities I'd once found so sought after. Betrayed by my fellow teachers, who seemed to be making the adjustment without a lot of grief. I felt like a visitor in a foreign country. Not only did I not understand the language being spoken, but I wasn't sure I really wanted to learn. I was sickened by the realization that I was now one of the "older" teachers who couldn't adapt to progress. The angrier I got, the less effective I became. When I listened to myself I sounded like the Grinch. Whining and complaining became my main form of communication.

It didn't take long for me to realize that something had to change. I was driving myself crazy, and driving my friends away. A more ambitious person may have decided to change the system. I must admit I thought about that, but I had to accept the fact that I had my hands full as it was. Maybe when the kids were grown and I'd been released from Relief Society.

No, the change had to come from within myself. I had to rearrange my expectations. Whereas teaching had at one time provided personal fulfillment and a creative outlet, it didn't now. That would have to be okay. After much soul-searching I admitted that I was teaching primarily because we needed the money. If I never got another positive stroke, another expression of effulgent gratitude, or another chance to show off, I'd survive. I'd still get my check at the end of the month.

Granted, that doesn't sound like a noble and lofty goal, and that attitude may shock those of you who like to think of public servants as tireless, dedicated, and self-sacrificing. The truth is that people in the helping professions are the most susceptible people in the world to job burnout, for a number of reasons. First, most of us *are* idealistic, and want, above all else, to make a difference in our environment. We've chosen our professions over more lucrative marketplace-oriented jobs because we want to improve the human condition. We're not emotionally prepared for the possibility of a stalemate, brought about by an overabundance of red tape, lack of funding for our save-the-world project, or the fact that humanity really isn't that excited about changing its condition. While we've always found our great sensitivity to be an advantage in our work, it turns on us when we find ourselves working under frustrating conditions. A less vulnerable person can say, "Well, that's how things are," and go on. A sensitive, change-the-world type can become overwhelmed when his attempts to reach success (according to his own definition of the word) are thwarted.

Someone has said, "When I accept myself as I am, I change, when I accept others the way they are, they change." I took that bit of insight a step further and proved that when I accepted my job the way it was, it changed.

The realization that I was working for a salary, not for personal gratification, was a necessary first step. From there I was able to make certain changes in myself. I realized that my

What in the Dickens Is Wrong with Great Expectations?   45

griping and bellyaching were contributing to my anxiety, not overcoming it, so I resolved not to engage in games of "Ain't It Awful" with other despairing teachers. Instead of adopting a self-righteous, Pollyanna attitude, I would simply respond to an invitation to commiserate by saying: "I've discovered that I just can't handle talking about it. I'll have to pass on that subject." Next I had to forget my own high hopes, at least for the time, and concentrate on teaching my students with love and as nearly Christlike an attitude as I could. You can guess the results. Some months after I'd decided to let go of the anger, I started getting the compliments and the appreciation I'd missed before. Still, the tributes were punctuated with kicks and shoves, and from time to time I've had to remind myself: The check is for the same amount on the months that they love you as on the months that they hate you.

Things won't stay the same. They can't. In time, if I keep growing in the right direction, I may discover ways to meet the requirements of the job and at the same time restructure some of its elements so it can better meet my needs. Or, I may reassess my needs. I may find another job more suited to my present skills. But none of these things will happen if I direct all my energies toward fighting. When I accept things as they are, I've discovered, they change.

Level of expectation plays a tremendous role in marriage burnout, parent burnout, and missionary burnout. Marriage, parenthood, and missionary work are presented in such glowing terms that they enjoy the same ethereal aura as Shangri-la and lemon puff pie. They're often linked with fantasies of instant joy and fail-proof fulfillment.

Marriage, parenthood, and missionary work are glorified because they are godly pursuits. I've got news for you lofty planners. Godhood is grueling, at least in the early stages of development. Anything worthy of our best endeavors holds the promise of joy beyond our capacity to experience it — peace, fulfillment, and all those good things. Remember that I've said that, because I may not repeat it. The task I've set for myself is to remind you of the opposition in all things. Before you can reach the heights you have to have established a more-than-casual relationship with the pits and the plains.

Not only do we expect marriage to be wonderful, but we expect our mate to have the same hopes, dreams, habits, and hang-ups as we do. After all, we chose him/her from among a cast of thousands, so it's *certainly* fair to assume that he or she can read our innermost thoughts and anticipate our every need. We expect that wives know how to be wives and that husbands know how to be husbands. We expect the same doting devotion we experienced on dates and the honeymoon to continue forever. We expect the impossible. Those who learn to revise their expectations survive marriage. Those who insist on having things the way they planned, or become shattered when the bubble bursts, burn out.

Parent burnout can occur for a number of reasons. Sometimes a parent expects a child to be something he isn't. When this happens, the kid burns out, because it's no fun sacrificing your own true self to satisfy somebody else's need for achievement, and the parent burns out when the kid suddenly discovers it's impossible to be something he isn't and either rebels, gets sick, or just becomes a dull, nowhere kid.

A fantastic number of parents of teenagers burn out because they expect appreciation. Some even expect to be treated like normal human beings! Others (foolish folk!) expect that they won't have to humbly eat the words they spoke so authoritatively when their children were little. "*My kids* will never let their rooms get in that condition!" "*My kids* will never look at me like that!" "What's wrong with those people that they allow their children to get away with such behavior!" "There must be something basically wrong in that home . . ."

Nowhere is the principle of expectation less understood and more misused than in the parent-child relationship. I'll bet you've heard a jillion times, "If you want your child to achieve, you must set high expectations for him." Okay, I'll go along with that. I guess, whether consciously or not, I've conveyed the message to my kids that I expect them to be honest, trustworthy, self-supporting (eventually), and to know the joy that comes with accomplishment. By allowing them to participate in a number of activities and by encouraging them to plan, design, and create, I'm saying to them: "I trust that you have the ability to do this. If you excel, you'll experience one

What in the Dickens Is Wrong with Great Expectations? 47

of the greatest feelings on earth. If you don't, you can still enjoy whatever level of proficiency you reach. If you botch it up beyond repair you can either try again or chalk it up to a bad experiment. You grow through learning; you learn by trying." The look of encouragement on my face and the note of confidence in my voice give the message, "I expect you to succeed, and on those unavoidable occasions when you don't I have confidence that you'll be able to handle the setback."

If I could afford to buy a full-page ad in your local newspaper, or if I had the nerve to rent a public address system and drive through town shouting with it, or if I could pull a Dr. Brothers routine and get on a talk show, I'd zealously proclaim that in most cases, your expectations for others should be general. When we get too specific about our plans for someone else's life we are toying with a sacred right, that of free agency. Here is a short list of common overly-specific expectations:

1. I expect you to be a doctor when you grow up. (Who cares that the kid has never passed a science class in his life and that he faints at the sight of blood? Doctors make good money, and they bring a lot of prestige to the family!)

2. I expect you to be first draft choice in the NFL as soon as you graduate from college with honors. (So the kid dreams of playing first violin in the middle school orchestra. What does he know? There's plenty of time for music in the next life. On the chance that they don't have Monday Night Football at that great Family Home Evening on high, you'd better have him go for the contact sports while he's in the flesh!)

3. I expect you to be married to a fine young returned missionary and to have presented me with at least three grandchildren by the time you're twenty-five. (A lot of variables working here. Will anyone ask her? If so, will it be someone she really wants to share her life with or "a nice guy, but definitely not The One?" And what if she can't have kids?)

When dealing with mates and offspring it's best to channel your expectations in the direction of unconditional positive regard. For example, "I expect you to live up to the best that's within you. I'll be in your corner to cheer you on, but I will neither push you nor limit you." It's tempting to want to control the life of someone you love. Resist the temptation and enrich the relationship.

Sandwiched somewhere between being a child and having one are the missionary years. I've never been a called missionary, so my musings on the subject may hold less conviction than do my heated harpings on the subjects of marriage and parenthood, but I have made several observations. One is that very few of the young men and women who serve as missionaries are prepared for the reality of missionary work. We form our opinions on the truly touching and beautiful report of the recently returned missionary who has, after much sweat and many tears, arrived at a level of spirituality that enables him to stand up in all honesty and with true conviction declare that the two years he spent in the mission field were, no doubt about it, the best two years of his life. Young marrieds don't stand up in church and declare that their first two years as man and wife were the best years of their lives! Devoted mothers rarely testify that the years between the two o'clock feedings and the two-year-old temper tantrums were the best of their lives, though looking back they may someday think they were. No occupation has been so completely and unanimously voted The Best as has missionary work. I'm sure it has something to do with the level of commitment demanded of a full-time missionary.

I sincerely believe the returnees when they apply superlatives to the time they spent as missionaries. But I find it equally easy to believe the young man who candidly admitted that yes, the missionary years had been his best, but they had also been his most difficult. It has to do with paying your dues. You have to come to a point that you are so filled with the Spirit that your joy is full. Reaching that point does not come painlessly. It involves work, fears, discouragement, and a lot of inconvenience. That spiritual high is not something they can quickly confer on you in the Missionary Training Center.

Whether you're reading this as an employee, a wife, a husband, a parent, or a potential missionary, I heartily encourage

What in the Dickens Is Wrong with Great Expectations? 49

you to harbor high hopes, dream delightful dreams, and, in general, expect the best. Happy, successful people live that way. Quite possibly the difference between a person who is consistently happy and successful and one who is happy only when his lofty demands are met is an ability (when all else fails) to roll with the punches, to redefine his goals. In a positive context the word *expectation* hints of a quality of freshness and embodies an element of surprise.

Excellence is almost always preceded by great expectations. Sometimes even fantastic expectations blossom into awesome achievements. Examine the quality of your expectations in terms of their effect on your outlook. *Great* expectations give you a feeling of excitement and personal potency. Destructive ones make you feel uptight and bogged down. While I'm not advocating that you always limit yourself to the obviously achievable, I do suggest that you develop at least a nodding acquaintance with reality.

Kid Burnout: The Problem

5

If you'd look at the 1979-80 edition of his high school annual, you'd read that Sean was voted Most Likely to Succeed. That year he made the all-state basketball team and was chosen to escort the queen at homecoming. His name frequently appeared on the honor roll. He was the kind of kid any parent would be proud to have. His teachers predicted future success in whatever field of endeavor Sean followed. His friends loved and admired him. Just about everyone wanted to be in his shoes.

If you'd look in the 1980-81 edition of his high school annual, you'd see an entire page dedicated to Sean. The page has a black border with a picture of Sean, smiling that irresistible smile, in the center. Under the picture is a memorial tribute to a beloved friend and an outstanding student. To the sickening shock and absolute disbelief of everyone who knew him, Sean shot himself one day. No one knew why.

Tina was a super student, too. She was the kind of girl who could participate in five events in a track meet one afternoon and look absolutely stunning at a beauty pageant that evening. She was pretty, talented, and smart. Her list of credits included honor roll, cheerleader, and track team. A lot of mothers wished their daughters could be more like Tina. That was

Kid Burnout: The Problem

before Tina changed. Almost overnight (or at least it seemed so to the casual observer) she went from a wholesome, happy young woman to a tormented, unmanageable rebel. Her parents blamed it on a boy she was dating. But why would a girl with so much going for her suddenly be so vulnerable?

Now that I've got your attention I'll admit that the examples I've used are extreme. Fortunately, teenage suicides are not common occurrences, but they are increasing at an alarming rate. Unfortunately, they do happen, and one teenage suicide is too many. Each case is different, and because of the finality of the act we don't think to ask why until it's too late. Fortunately, too, most young people who start out being good students and active participants reap many personal benefits from their work and experience a great deal of satisfaction from their achievements. Success builds upon success and life is a great adventure. But not always. *Kid burnout* is a colloquial term I use to describe a state of not-so-well-being in children and youth. I use the term *kid* because it's so general. I can use one word to refer to an eighteen-year-old and a preschooler alike. I use *burnout* to replace the clinical terms *depression, anxiety,* and *stress.*

I'll take the liberty of lumping depression, anxiety, and stress together for this presentation because there is so much overlap in the way they manifest themselves and, more importantly, in how to deal with them. By no means do I wish to rob the clinician of his right to differentiate among the three states. Because I'm trying to cover an involved and controversial subject in two chapters I plead guilty to the charge of oversimplification.

Stress is a recently popularized concept and deals with the interaction of the body with the emotions. Some stress is necessary for achievement, and healthy stress is an important component of a full life. Too much stress, on the other hand, can be the cause of some of the problems we will discuss here. Anxiety more specifically deals with fear, dread, and apprehension, but is usually caused by a mingling of the hang-ups of the day, be they guilt, anger, or whatever. Depression is what often happens when anxiety is too painful to tolerate. When depression takes over the feeling of uptightness is replaced by a feeling of nothingness. We often relate depression to feelings of extreme boredom, emptiness, isolation, and alienation. Some psychologists say that childhood/youth depression is almost always masked or disguised. Its disguises are often the same symptoms attributed to stress and anxiety.

Only recently has the literature recognized the fact that stress and depression really exist in young people. *Youth* has always been linked with words like *carefree, happy-go-lucky,* and *lighthearted.* Maybe we're forced to come face-to-face with the reality of stress and anxiety in young people because of today's achievement-oriented society and its unprecedented pressures. On the other hand, maybe it's just that adults are more sensitive than they used to be. I wept as I shared this poem with my eighteen-year-old who, as any eighteen-year-old would, understand its message only too well.

Youth

You see youth as a joyous thing
About whom love and laughter cling.
You see youth as a joyous elf
Who sings sweet songs to please himself.
You see his laughing, sparkling eyes
To take earth's wonders with surprise.
You think him free from cares and woes,
And naught of fear you think he knows,
You see him tall, naively bold.
You see him thus, for you are old.

But I, I see him otherwise,
An unknown fear within his eyes.
He works and plays and never knows
Where he is called nor why he goes.
Each youth sustains within his breast
A vague and infinite unrest.
He goes about in still alarm,
With shrouded future at his arm,
With longings that can find no tongue.
I see him thus, for I am young.[1]

---

1. From Mother Education lesson no. 9, "Too Much Pressure?" *Relief Society Course of Study: 1985* (Salt Lake City: The Church of Jesus Christ of Latter-day Saints).

Kid Burnout: The Problem

To oversimplify again, and to borrow terms which are likely to be familiar to you, the burned-out kid is one who feels "not okay," who thinks of himself as not loveable and capable, or who feels powerless to control his own life. A self-protecting, face-saving kid would never want to admit to such feelings, so he unconsciously chooses his own style of defense. He may get sick. Really sick, not put-on sick, although his illness may be completely emotionally based. It's easy to diagnose the old stomachache-on-the-day-of-a-test routine, but burned-out kids can develop symptoms that don't really seem to be associated with anything. Headaches and stomachaches are popular psychosomatic ailments. So are changes in eating habits, ranging from a sudden tendency to eat compulsively to a potentially life-threatening case of anorexia. Ulcers, colitis, and asthma are common stress-related conditions. The young person who is unhappy or anxiety ridden is more susceptible to any disease than is one who is generally happy and on top of things.

Kid burnout can also manifest itself as a phobia. School phobia is not uncommon, and it's no respecter of age. A few years ago I did an internship in a residential school for disturbed adolescents. Most of the kids made it pretty obvious why they were there. Some were there as a halfway measure between the youth detention center and their homes. Others didn't have homes. One or two of the kids were mentally retarded, and some were drug addicts. There was a lot of street language and acting out, so one of the girls, who engaged in none of this, stuck out like a sore thumb. She was bright, extremely talented, and very well behaved. When I asked why in the world she was there, the director told me that she had just quit going to school. Obviously her parents felt that a residential school was better than no school at all. I reacted like you are probably reacting. *Crazy kid,* I thought, *certainly Inglewood* (I knew her school, and it wasn't that bad) *was better than this!* But the truth is, to the severely depressed youth it isn't a matter of not wanting to get up and go to school, it's a matter of not being able to. And when depression has reached this point, no amount of advice to get hold of yourself, set goals, and think positive will do any good. A depressed kid will often be so worried about the inevitable coming of the next day that he can't go to sleep at night.[2] Depressed people commonly can't sleep when they want to and can't stay awake when they are supposed to.

I saw the other end of the age continuum at my school this year. My classroom is on the same hall as one of the kindergarten classes. The other day (and this was in May!) I was rushing down the hall at about 8:15 (school starts at 8:00) and I saw the most pitiful-looking little child I've ever seen. His pace would have made a snail look hyperactive by comparison, and next to his scowl Jack Palance would have looked like a candidate to play the leading role in *Son of Pollyanna*. Not knowing his story, and thinking he had lost his lunch money or been bitten by the mangy dog that sometimes hangs around the school, I asked what was wrong. The boy glared at me, wiped a tear from his eye, and said flatly, "I hate school." I then went to the office and saw a woman I knew had to be his mother. Looking guilty and spent she filled me in. Walking from the office to his classroom was a real breakthrough for the kid. His mother had had to physically tear herself free from his grip and play the tough guy before the boy would begin the terrible trudge from the front of the building to his classroom, where he would join two charming teachers and a group of children, playing delightedly with blocks and Legos.

Hostility is another mask for depression (or another dress for stress). Unfortunately for us parents, the burned-out kid usually directs his hostility toward the person or persons closest to him. I don't mean to imply that just because your teenager occasionally acts like you are the biggest fool or the meanest monster in the world that he is seriously depressed or overstressed. Anyone who has reared a child to the age of fifteen or more is familiar with a sporadic spewing of accusations or an occasional outpouring of put-downs. Those of us who have parented teenagers have of necessity either cried bucketfuls of tears or developed a thick skin that would make even a

---

2. If you can feel your blood pressure rising in your veins and you want to shout, "Whadda ya mean, not able to and can't?" you're a prime candidate to be a contributor to youth burnout. Of course he's able to go to school, if able means knowing how to put one foot on the floor, then the next, etc. But the feeling I describe is real, unacceptable as it may seem.

Kid Burnout: The Problem

well-dressed alligator look vulnerable. Kids have to assert their independence, and somehow convincing themselves that their parents are incompetent oafs is the most natural way to do it. The time to start thinking that something more serious is happening is the time that the eruptions of ugliness are not interspersed with moments of closeness and expressions of love, however well disguised they may be. When you, a pillar of strength and a fountain of compassion, find yourself wanting to retaliate, there's a good chance that there's something more serious than a developmental stage underlying the displays of anger.

Often young people act out when they are overcome with anxiety or despair. Acting out means simply doing things that they know are against our value system. Lying, stealing, and acting silly or disrespectful in school are common manifestations of burnout in young children.

Unhappy adolescents are vulnerable to drugs and drinking, not just because they want to rebel but because the mind-altering substances offer them a chance to escape from the pain they are experiencing. Sex holds an attraction for the youth with low self-esteem, especially if he feels isolated or alienated. Often it is not sex itself which is so attractive, but the attempt on the part of the young person to align himself with someone to fill the emotional void inside. Reckless or drunk driving may indicate that the youth would just as soon risk death as cope with life.

School problems are often an indication of burnout. In adolescents and young adults failure to take final exams, frequent changing of courses of study, changing from full-time to part-time schooling, and, of course, dropping out of school are clues that all is not well. Scores of children manifest their discouragement by becoming what we know as underachievers. Others are hyperactive.

Underachievement is such a common problem in school-age children that I tend to get soap-boxy about it. I have to bridle myself and point out, though, that underachieving behavior can indicate a number of things. First of all, the term *underachievement* implies that we are omniscient and know what the child in question is capable of achieving. It's downright hypocritical to assume that a child is capable of achieving at a certain level just because he looks intelligent and has certain skills. An IQ score helps teachers and parents to make an educated guess, but sometimes even an IQ score provides only a rough index. Assuming that the test score is a valid indication of the kid's ability, a student can be said to be an underachiever if his standard scores on achievement tests are significantly lower than his IQ score. A kid with an IQ of 100 should be achieving at right about grade level. A kid with an IQ score of 90 would be expected to achieve a little below grade level, and one with an IQ of, say, 120, should be achieving above grade level (if your school allows him that privilege). Your school counselor, psychologist, or special education teacher can show you how to compare test scores. Once you've established that your child is achieving below his expected level, the obvious task is to determine why. The world is full of cut-and-dried answers, and it's important that you look at all the possibilities before you buy any of them. For example, does this profile look familiar?

Fred is the classic underachiever. His teachers are convinced that his only problem is laziness. "He has the ability . . . !" His parents give up. They are tired of hearing teachers complain about Fred's poor work habits, because they can't seem to make a difference. They've tried everything, and nothing seems to help.

Fred seldom finishes his work. His desk is a disaster, as is his room at home. He daydreams. He makes excuses. He's not belligerent, but he can lead his teachers to the point of explosion, the way he sits in class and does nothing. He's beginning to get a reputation as a "dumb kid" because of the way he acts at school.

Most schools are full of kids like Fred, and almost as full of adults ready to put a label on problems like Fred's. But that can't be done readily. This profile could be that of an anxious child, or a depressed child, or a child with an attention deficit. Or it may be that Fred's style of thinking is so different from that of his teacher that the two minds never meet! Or it may be all of the above. Fred may have an attention deficit and have become so frustrated by the futility of trying to achieve with-

Kid Burnout: The Problem 57

out the necessary skills that he has become anxious or depressed.

No matter what Fred's problem he will undoubtedly profit from the unconditional love, self-esteem building suggestions I offer in the next chapter. Still, if he has an attention deficit, he may need additional help. If Fred's behavior is interfering seriously with his school progress or causing him to lose confidence in himself, you owe it to him to cover all the bases.

Kids who are working significantly below grade level will probably be identified and evaluated by the school. Bear in mind, though, that what is significant to you, with your high standards of achievement, may not be significant to the teacher, who is comparing your child to kids who may have much more serious problems. Ask your child's teacher how she sees the situation. If she can't answer your questions to your satisfaction she will probably refer you to the school counselor, the student support team, one of the special education teachers, or the principal. Each school system has its own referral system.

Our school works this way. (If you're in the United States yours will probably have the same general hierarchy, because federal legislation has quite a bit to say about how special programs are handled in the school. There will undoubtedly be some superficial differences.) Either a teacher or a parent can refer a student to the student support team, which is made up of a small group of classroom teachers, special education teachers, and administrators, for evaluation. The student is observed, interviewed, and given some achievement tests. He is also given a screening test to determine his mental age or IQ range. The school psychologist reviews this data. If the child's problem is seen to be serious enough that it is interfering significantly with his ability to succeed in school the psychologist will, with your permission, administer a battery of tests, usually including the WISC-R (revised edition of the Weschler Intelligence Tests for Children). Most psychologists choose this test because it not only provides an IQ (intelligence quotient), but it also provides subtests and verbal and performance indices which will help the psychologist to determine the specific nature of the child's problem.

If the psychologist decides that your child's problem is not interfering with his school success to such a degree that testing is warranted and you feel strongly that it is, of course you can protest. But be reasonable. While it would be great if every kid with a problem could be tested, most school systems can't afford the personnel to make this option available. If you think, *Well, maybe my kid doesn't fit their standards of severity, but it's serious to me,* find a competent psychologist (those associated with reputable universities are usually a safe bet) and get your child tested. It will be expensive, but it will be worth it in terms of peace of mind.

You could engage the best psychologist in town, and there would still be some subjectivity involved. Sometimes a judgment between a diagnosis of "attention deficit" and "anxiety" is based on observation of behavior, and two psychologists could come up with different conclusions on the same kid. My advice is, after you have your child tested, follow the psychologist's recommendations. Give yourself a few months to evaluate their effectiveness. Then if things don't get better, make a follow-up appointment. You may think you are following the recommendations implicitly, but you may be overlooking something or giving some wrong messages without even knowing it. If that doesn't help, maybe a second opinion is indicated. The behavioral sciences are not exact sciences, and standardized tests are not scripture.

I put you through all that because I often get zealous and link anxiety with underachievement to the exclusion of the other possibilities. I wanted to point out that anxiety-based behavior and attention-deficit behavior are often so similar that they baffle the best. I don't want anyone to make a snap judgment on my account. The message I want to convey is that behavior like Fred's—which is often described colloquially and judgmentally as lazy, not working to capacity, flaky, spacey, and disorganized—can be a manifestation of kid burnout, or, in other words, stress, anxiety, or depression. When this is the case, the things parents and teachers commonly do to "discipline" kids like Fred only compound the problem.

We all love our kids and want what's best for them. To most of us the ability to give Christlike, unconditional love

Kid Burnout: The Problem

does not come naturally. Most of us unconsciously choose the way we show love according to (1) the way our own parents showed their love to us and (2) our own needs. Most of us (and by "us" I mean the conscientious, family-centered people of this world who want, above all, to be good parents and good people) do whatever we do because we honestly believe it's in our kids' best interests. But for all our good intentions we occasionally discover that our kids don't respond to our love and discipline the way they are "supposed to." While one kid seems to blossom under our style of parenting, another may rebel, withdraw, or otherwise show that he just can't cope. When this happens it's good to look at what we are doing and how it may be affecting the kid in question.

Most of us conscientious, "mature," family-oriented parents err, when we do err, by being either demanding or overprotective. "Who, me?" you ask. Take overprotective, for example. Many of us would go into orbit if anyone called us by that name! Some of us overprotect our kids because we are not sure of ourselves and we think the way to provide a secure childhood (and that is certainly a goal worth striving for) is to make sure our kids never have any negative experiences. Or we just can't stand to hear them cry! Some parents are overly solicitous of their children because they feel guilty for causing them pain. Divorced mothers sometimes fall into this trap. Others were overprotected themselves, and they are modeling their own parents' behavior.

You are not being overprotective just because you don't allow your fourteen-year-old to go to the rock concert (although he'll try everything he can think of to convince you that you are). In fact, you might be being overprotective if you *do* let your fourteen-year-old go to the rock concert, because sometimes overindulgent is overprotective. One mistake the overprotective parent makes is that of not allowing her[3] child to experience reality. If a kid gets a candy bar whenever he and his mom are out shopping and he asks for one, he's overpro-

---

3. I've sex-stereotyped here, because it's more common for a mother to be overprotective and a father to be demanding, although it is by no means always that way.

tected. If a mother says she'll take the kids to the park when they get their rooms cleaned, but she takes them before their rooms are cleaned because it will soon be dark and they are tired, she's overprotective. If a parent repeatedly takes a forgotten lunch or book bag to school, she's overprotective. Sometimes mothers are overprotective to compensate for fathers who are too demanding, and vice versa.

Overprotective is not allowing your child to do the task he is able to do at any given stage of development. When a kid is old enough to pour his own milk but you insist on pouring his milk for him, he gets the idea that he is too clumsy or too helpless to pour milk. If all the other kids his age ride their bikes to the neighborhood store but you are afraid yours will get hurt, your kid may question his ability to take responsibility for himself, or he may develop a crippling fear of accidents. If you tell your kid what to wear every morning, he won't develop a lot of confidence in his ability to make a decision. If you continually answer questions directed toward your child he'll think there's something wrong with the way he talks. If you're always available to fix a snack or to iron a shirt on demand, you're giving your kids permission to tyrannize you (or their future wives or husbands), even when they're grown and strong and you're old and tired.

As kids get older we overprotect them by worrying and reminding. In our family we joke about the Mormon Goodbye, "Remember who you are and what you represent." While the advice is timely and the message carries a depth that we would all do well to contemplate, I have reservations about repeating it every time a kid leaves the house. I believe that when you continually remind him, you are assuming that he will forget who he is and what he represents unless you draw it to his attention. I mentioned this to a group of mothers of my daughter's friends, and one woman said, "I feel that if I don't say it to my kids, I'm not being a good mother!" I laughed, because I suddenly realized that I feel exactly the same way about the phrase, "Be careful."

Especially on a rainy or snowy night, or when one of my kids is going to drive a long distance, or do anything risky (or fun) like water ski or shoot rapids, I just can't resist the

Kid Burnout: The Problem

impulse. I'd never forgive myself if I didn't say "Be careful," and then something happened! As if my kids were stupid enough or impulsive enough that they wouldn't think to be careful without my reminder. Or, as if they would be any more careful with it! That's overprotective. While this kind of reminding will probably fall in the category of "Oh, Mother! (sigh)" and not do much permanent damage, if the worrying mother is apprehensive enough to transmit her anxiety, she is teaching her child to be fearful and unsure of himself.

Smothering is close to overprotective. The smothering parent is one who lacks so much attention/affection herself that she resents the child's natural attempt to form other close relationships or to become independent. Smothering can be obvious or subtle, but it always makes itself felt. Even being in the same room with a smotherer can make one feel emotionally drained and very inhibited. The smotheree often has to fight inwardly to maintain his own individuality and sense of direction.

While the overprotective parent may need love and attention from his child, the demanding parent often needs validation from his. In other words, he sees his child as an extension of himself, and if his kid doesn't look good, he doesn't look good. He feels it is his duty to remind, to direct—okay, I'll say it—to "control" his child. With the very best of intentions, to be sure. Most demanding parents are only modeling what they learned from their parents before them, and they honestly believe it is their responsibility to "stay on top of" their kids at all times: to correct them, to push them, to make plans for them, and to set goals for them. They find it extremely difficult to trust their kids to make their own decisions and plan their own time. As with the overprotective parent, the demanding parent is usually very concerned and conscientious.

We all parent in a way that is natural for us, and we will continue to do so until we discover that what we are doing doesn't work. Actually, while I had no problem with the term *overprotective* (I mean, after all, doesn't *protective* have a warm, motherly feel to it? The *over* is just a matter of degree . . .), I don't like the word *demanding*, because it seems to have a judgmental ring. Maybe *authoritarian* is more acceptable. Semantically, I may be in trouble. Aren't Latter-day Saint parents, especially fathers, supposed to be authoritarian? The answer to that one is obvious to the student of scripture. Yes, the head of the home has, and is meant to exercise, authority. No, he shouldn't necessarily be *authoritarian* as the term is commonly used:

> No power or influence can or ought to be maintained by virtue of the priesthood, only by persuasion, by long-suffering, by gentleness and meekness, and by love unfeigned;
> By kindness, and pure knowledge, which shall greatly enlarge the soul without hypocrisy, and without guile. (D&C 121: 41–42.)

Sometimes a parent can be demanding without meaning to be. Occasionally I see a child whose parents seem to be accepting, low-key, and loving, but the child seems to be under a great deal of pressure to succeed. When parents are very successful and achievement-oriented themselves a sensitive child may read this message: "My parents value achievement highly. Therefore, in order to please them (be accepted by them, be worthy of them), I must achieve great things." Some children not only need not to be pushed, they also need to be taught specifically that they are loved for themselves and not for their accomplishments.

The examples I used at the beginning of the chapter, those of Sean and Tina, don't, on the surface, seem to be very good examples of burned-out kids, do they? Unfortunately, though, I've seen very similar real life examples. I've seen an entire community shocked by the suicide of an apparently happy and very successful and popular teenager. I've seen kids go from radiant and successful to sullen and belligerent in a short period of time.

Some would point to a genetic weakness; others to a character flaw. Still others would use descriptive labels like "depressive reaction to adolescence" or look at life-stress situations. Any of these are possible explanations for suicidal or acting out behavior. We do have certain research-supported facts about the cause of severe depression in young people. For instance, many depressed kids have depressed parents. A child

Kid Burnout: The Problem

who has been separated from an important loved one, such as a mother, for periods of several months or more during the early years of life has an increased vulnerability to depression. Sometimes a single episode of depression can be traced to the loss of an important loved one: divorce of parents, the death of a close and supportive parent, a move, or the breakup of a boy-girl relationship. Kids who have to deal with a serious illness or disability in themselves or a close family member are more susceptible to depression than are those with no serious health problems. Then there are the causes of burnout I mentioned in an earlier chapter: *A lack of balance. Being guided by a driving force, rather than a rational plan. Being guided from without, rather than from within. Discovering that the rewards of a given task (or life) are not commensurate with the energy expended.*

It's possible that while Sean and Tina were outwardly well-adjusted and happy there were some areas of their lives that were lacking. They managed to adapt on the outside, but at some point in their lives the strain under which they were living became too much to handle. While their lives appeared to be well-balanced (they were active in all areas — intellectual, physical, cultural, and religious), they seem not to have had the emotional and spiritual strength necessary to help them over the rough spots. To a young person without a strong base of self-esteem a life crisis, such as the death of a loved one or a major disappointment, could prove devastating.

Kids, especially those who have not grown up with unconditional love, will go to great lengths for love and approval. Parents (sometimes unconsciously) may be so anxious to teach their children to be successful that they reward success and punish failure to the extent that their children start believing that when they are not doing something outstanding or praiseworthy, they are not worthwhile. Children who hold this belief will push themselves relentlessly *(being guided by a driving force)* to accomplish, thinking that this is the only way to be loved. Having never learned that they are lovable with or without their achievements, they never learn to give *themselves* unconditional love. Their accomplishments are empty, because they are never enough.

The parent who feels it is his responsibility to push his child to success is like the owner of the old and uncooperative horse —he believes that the only way to keep his child moving is to constantly keep the carrot (his approval) just out of reach. "Good. You've done that, now see if you can do this!" The child never learns to sit back, pat himself on the back, and say, "Boy, that achievement felt good!" He is always under pressure. He feels a constant need to produce. He does what he does to please others, not because it's his idea of an exciting, fulfilling life. There is always the fear that if he *doesn't* succeed, the approval of his parents (and by this time it will have generalized to his friends, his teachers, his advisors, etc.) will be taken away. The thought could be devastating. A child (or an adult, for that matter) who lives life for the approval of others is likely to lose sight of his authentic or inner self, which is that spirit he brought with him from the premortal existence. While he will use some of his natural talents to bring about his great achievements, he will undoubtedly ignore others, those which are not so highly valued by his parents or teachers. Ignoring your uniqueness is a step in the direction of spiritual death, or, more directly and descriptively, of an emotional deadness—depression.

Young and old, we all need to experience a feeling of power over our own lives. The youth who doesn't feel secure in his sense of power may appear irresponsible, because he hasn't developed a healthy sense of responsibility for himself. He may act helpless or he may be excessively demanding or stubborn. He may be overly compliant or he may show a lack of emotional control. When the youth sees his parents as exercising a dampening influence on his ability to control his own life he may look for an excuse to leave home—if not physically, then emotionally. Occasionally the kid who rebels bigtime may do so because that is the only way he can see to assert his independence. Both overprotecting and overcontrolling parents can rob a child of his sense of power.

It's my belief that the difference between the Seans and Tinas of the world and those young people who enjoy their successes and somehow muddle through their setbacks is that the Seans and Tinas never developed the love for self that

Kid Burnout: The Problem

tends to enhance the peaks and pad the valleys. Kids like Fred have made the decision that just not trying is better than opening themselves to the humiliation of trying and failing. Burned-out kids probably don't know why they feel a constant ache or emptiness inside. They may not even know that it's okay to talk about it. Their only hope may be a parent who is concerned enough to stop what he's doing and look at some new ways of loving or listening, or a teacher who is willing to look below the protective cover and see a vulnerable, frightened child.

I'd be willing to bet that you'll see a burned-out kid within the week, if not within the day. Can you resist the opportunity to help?

Kid Burnout: 6
The Solution

To Parents and Teachers:

When I decided I wanted to be a writer my life underwent a gradual change. I discovered that in order to write I needed a block of time—alone. I further discovered that in order to get that block of time I had to learn to say no, to ignore, and, well, sometimes, to get right tough about it. I became protective, maybe defensive, about my time and my right to control it. I wish I could say it was all for the best, but my determination took its toll. I lost a few friends. I guess I also lost some of my spontaneity. I'm still looking for the balance between protecting my space and reaching out to others.

The problem complicated itself when I started teaching full-time. It wasn't long before I discovered that I was not one of those superachievers you read about in *Working Woman*, and that there was no way for me to be a worker, wife, mother, Mormon, and writer at the same time. Then I became a summer writer. I vowed that during my two and one-half months of vacation I would work seven hours a day on my writing, with the exception of weekends and holidays. It sounded like a good idea at the time.

A year previous to the time I write this I was in our ward Relief Society presidency. We received word that our ward

Kid Burnout: The Solution											67

had been asked to host a group of Church members from the Dominican Republic who were coming to Atlanta to go to the temple. The host family was to house, feed, transport, and entertain the family assigned to them for the four days that they were here. It sounded like a big job.

I can still remember my feelings when the sign-up sheet came to me. I was torn. I had just started writing this book and I was anxious to get on with it. I had scheduled every minute of every day, and I wanted to keep on schedule. I was a little irritated that something had come up to interfere with my timetable. If I hadn't been in a position of leadership it would have been easy for me to pass the sign-up sheet on without even getting out my reading glasses. But I'm big on setting examples. I signed, reluctantly.

The project turned out to be even more time consuming than I had expected. For the four days that our guests were here I cooked, I drove, I sightsaw, I even spent the few hours I had left helping in the temple youth center. But I never resented a minute. That four days will go down in my history as one of the peak experiences of my life. Never before have I encountered such love, such appreciation, such understanding (especially considering that our communication consisted of a few phrases I had picked up in Spanish 101 twenty years ago and a lot of ridiculous-looking gestures), and such undiluted spirituality. I know for sure that the feeling I experienced on those hot July days is the same one that permeates the celestial kingdom.

This year another group of Dominicans came to the temple. There were fewer families coming and more families wanting to host, so they didn't send around a sign-up sheet; they just announced that anyone who was interested should see Brother Kinghorn. I was first in line to sign up. Again, it would mean I'd have to give up my sacred schedule, and that I'd have to take a week's vacation from my writing. But this time I knew what I'd be missing if I didn't host a family. Accomplishments seemed insignificant when compared with that spiritual high.

I wasn't disappointed. This time I didn't even *try* to accomplish anything while they were here, I just rolled with the punches and enjoyed the experience. After my houseguests left

I went back to my writing. This chapter, I'd decided, would be centered on unconditional love, as that was the best antidote I'd been able to find for youth burnout. I went back to my research—reading everything I could find on the subject of unconditional love.

I was amazed to discover that the feeling I had associated with hosting the Dominicans was exactly the feeling I was reading about. Partly because of the nature of the relationship and partly because of the personal attributes of our guests, I had recently experienced most of the components of unconditional (you can also call it celestial) love:

1. Love[1] lives in the here and now. (Our situation was, of course, ideal for that. With my new friends there were no past hurts to forgive and no worries about the future.)

2. Love accepts others as they are without wanting to change them. Love is nonjudgmental.

3. Love does not wish to control another person.

4. Love is related to trust. Love does not need to control circumstances.

5. Love does not use labels to categorize people.

6. Love is responsible.

7. Love is spontaneous.

8. Love strives for perfection, but neither needs it in oneself nor demands it in others.

9. Love is constantly growing, changing, taking risks.

10. Love recognizes needs, in oneself and in others.

11. Love is free from guilt and fear.

12. The loving person has a healthy concern for self.

13. The loving person is guided by the inner self, the spiritual self. This guidance occasionally transcends logic.

14. The loving person feels a sense of unity with all mankind.

I can hear you now. "My kid is burning out before my eyes! And now this author promises me a solution, then she gets on a tangent about some people from the Dominican Republic on a temple trip! What does that have to do with kid burnout?"

---

1. To avoid being out-and-out redundant, in this list I'll use the word *love* to mean *unconditional love*.

Kid Burnout: The Solution

I mentioned this experience in the hope that you will be able to recall a similar experience in your life. One where you felt at one with God and humanity. Remember how it felt. How it tasted. It can be a short-lived experience, like a testimony meeting or a telephone conversation, or it can span a long period of time, like the two years you spent as a missionary in Samoa. Relish the memory, and compare your state of mind during that time to the fourteen points listed above.

For years I've been running around telling parents and teachers that the best way to fight kid burnout is through the use of unconditional love. By that I meant that kids have to know that we love them with or without their accomplishments, that while we certainly share their joy in their achievements we must more importantly let them know that it is they themselves that we love. For example, "I'm delighted that you got an *A* in math. I know you worked hard for it, and I know it's a great feeling. I'd be dishonest if I didn't say it makes me proud when I see you doing so well in school. But you know, I love you just because you're you, no matter what your math grade is!" Kids have to be reminded constantly that they're loved just because they're loveable, and they're loveable just because they're them.

I still say that, because it's still true, but I go beyond that now. Having grown up with my kids, and having watched a lot of other people grow up with theirs, I've come to realize that our kids are not so much a product of what we say as of what we do, and not so much of what we do as of what we are. When we say one thing and project another, kids get mixed messages, and mixed messages can drive a kid crazy. Unless you actually do accept your kid as he is, it won't do much good to tell him you do. Unless you accept yourself as you are, it will be difficult for you to accept your kids (husband, wife, friends, parents . . .) as they are. For some of us it takes a real spiritual conversion before we can accept ourselves and others unconditionally. For most of us that spiritual conversion is a life's work. But it's never too soon or too late to begin.

Unconditional love, I've discovered, is a state-of-being synonomous with "true spirituality" and "mental health" and any other label you can find that means a divinely inspired sense of well-being. It must contain an element of the divine; otherwise it contradicts itself. Take concern for self as an example. People who have never experienced a true, divinely-centered love for self are quick to point out that it is vain, conceited, and selfish to love oneself, and that those who love themselves are (to use a fondly remembered Draper, Utah, expression) not worth shooting. The truth is that people who flaunt their assets obnoxiously are those who, in reality, hold themselves in low esteem. They continually try to convince themselves and others of their own importance. Truly confident people don't need to be reassured.

If all of us were completely confident of our loveability and capability we wouldn't need our children to validate us. We would be able to love them always, protect them when they needed protecting, and free them to be themselves. Look at the way our Savior loves us. He wraps us in his love, which assures us that we will never be given any challenge too great for us. But he is neither overly demanding nor overprotective. He outlines the rules for progression clearly, yet he lets us know that he will always accept and love us even if we fail miserably. Unlike many mortal parents he doesn't try to shield his children from growth-producing adventures, even when they involve some pain.

Most of us inherit the "good parent" conscience which makes us think that we're not doing our duty unless we nag, punish, legislate, and control. Because it *is* our responsibility to teach and guide our children, and because kids *do* need a certain amount of structure in their lives, we may resort to "control" tactics because that's the only way we know to offer guidance. We can't measure discipline and advice in pounds and ounces and say, "Give this much but no more." Because we are all influenced so much by our own backgrounds and experiences, and because no two parents think the same, we can't always rely on our powers of reasoning to tell us what approach is best to use with which kid at any given time.

Unconditional love, as the Savior taught it, is (so far as I can determine) the only fool-proof plan for successful parenting. However, if most of us waited until we had mastered the use of it, we would be putting off having children until the

Kid Burnout: The Solution

eternities. The important thing is that we continue (begin?) to progress in that direction. I certainly don't know everything there is to know about it, and I know a lot more than I practice. No matter how much or how little one understands, words are a poor vehicle in which to convey that understanding. It's my belief that no one can comprehend a relationship with Jesus Christ, which I believe is synonomous with unconditional love as I describe it, without a *tremendous desire* to do so.

I guess there are some people who are so hungry for righteousness that they possess this desire even when they're well and happy. But I'm not one of them. I had to become so uncomfortable with my boring, compulsive life-style that total commitment was the only viable option. I had to be so desperate for peace of mind that I was willing to give it all up (all the pride, the arrogance, the fear, and the anger) and submit myself to the will of God.

Pretty heavy. But as I said, words are inadequate tools; the task is not nearly as formidable as it may sound. Mine was not a sinner-to-saint conversion as we think of one, so a few less frown wrinkles are my only outward proof of progress. I was baptized at age eight, and I've never failed a temple recommend interview. I was active in the Church and looked okay on the surface, but things just weren't working for me. I was fat. I was tired. I was discouraged. Getting up in the morning was next to death on my list of desirable activities—some mornings death didn't look that bad compared to the alternative. I had a great family, but I wasn't enjoying them as I wanted to, and I knew I wasn't giving them the best I had to give. I had sunk about as low as I cared to go.

I had heard about the "rebirth of the spirit," and "total commitment," and I'd always sort of felt like everyone knew something that I didn't know. Here I was an adult, and I'd held a lot of responsible positions in the Church, and when someone would talk about sanctification or a relationship with the Savior I would secretly wonder if I'd missed something along the way. I've had that feeling in a placement committee meeting at school or in a graduate seminar, when someone would suddenly start throwing around a new psychological or educational term that I had never heard in my life. Of course I wasn't going to *admit* my ignorance—I just kept my mouth shut and hoped no one would blow my cover.

I handled my spiritual progression, or lack of it, pretty much the same way. I have always felt that it was wrong to seek a spiritual experience just for the sake of having a spiritual experience, and who knows, maybe I was afraid that if I pushed it too far I'd be shaken up like Saul on the road to Damascus or like Alma the Younger and the sons of Mosiah. The truth is, except for the occasional uneasy feeling that I was missing out on something, I really didn't feel the *need* for a rebirth of my spirit. I'd been baptized and confirmed, hadn't I?

Even after I became so bogged down and unhappy I fought making the commitment. The way to "at-one-ment," I'd heard, was to learn to completely submit yourself to the Lord. That terrified me. I've always had an authority problem. The worst thing I can think of is to lose my autonomy. I'd worked all these years to get control of my life, and then, *lose it?* Willingly? I'd never had any question about keeping the commandments, and the Word of Wisdom had always made sense. But my time was another matter. *Surrender it?*

At first I had to pray that I would be able to make the commitment. "Help me to be willing to place my life in thy hands" came long before "thy will be done." I still phase in and out of willingness; I guess most of us do. But when I am in tune I know that my fears were (are) completely groundless—ridiculous, even. The Lord didn't choose to replace my sense of humor with solemnity—he gave me the ability to laugh at myself. He didn't give me a list of boring tasks to perform—he gave me the ability to enjoy everything I have to do. He didn't put me in a role as "Super Mom"—he showed me that only as I enrich my own life can I enrich the lives of my family. He hasn't made the task of parenting easy, and I don't think he intends to. But he has called my attention to the fact that when I am angry or overprotective toward my children I am not acting in his name, and he has given me the words of Joseph Smith to display prominently on my refrigerator door:

> No thing is so much calculated to lead people to forsake sin as to take them by the hand, and watch over them with tenderness.

Kid Burnout: The Solution   73

> When persons manifest the least kindness and love to me, O
> what power it has over my mind, while the opposite course has a
> tendency to harrow up all the harsh feelings and depress the
> human mind.[1]

I have three reasons for relating the importance of a
spiritual rebirth to effective parenting. The first is, your weaknesses may not be the same as mine. Whereas I was inspired to
look to my own emotional and social needs, someone who
reads this may be overemphasizing their own development
and actually neglecting their children. I don't know how many
times I've been teaching a class or conducting a workshop and
found myself stressing an idea only to discover that someone
in the class needed to hear the exact opposite. In school and in
church we emphasize the importance of teaching the individual. While we humans can work at this, and it's important that
we do, only the Holy Ghost has perfected the art. While we
are responsible to obtain as much education as we can from
books and institutions, it's a good idea to have our new insights validated (or voided) by the Spirit.

Second, I feel fairly safe in making this prediction: Those
of you who have a natural tendency to be guided by emotion
or spirituality will look at my observations and suggestions
and think, *Hey, that makes sense!* Those of you, on the other
hand, who think in a more concrete way, who put a lot of
importance on structure, logic, and reality, are likely to think
(if, by some quirk of fate, you find yourself even reading
material such as this), *This lady is a real soft touch!* I know
from my own experience that the precepts and practices that I
needed to learn the most were the most difficult for me to
assimilate. When the suggestion that I might be doing something wrong came from another human being I fought it frantically. When the direction came from the Spirit I eventually
had to accept it. The Spirit will teach you, step by step, as you
increase in your ability to grasp and implement ideas, things
that another human being may not have the skill nor the
patience to help you to learn. You can't go too far to one
extreme or the other if you are open to personal revelation.

---

1. *Teachings of the Prophet Joseph Smith,* comp. Joseph Fielding Smith (Salt
Lake City: Deseret Book Co., 1938), p. 240.

Third, when you learn unconditional love from a spiritual interaction with your Father in Heaven, who is the source of love, a change takes place that is more than a mere assimilation of ideas. Your emotions are educated, not only your intellect. While it will still take practice and a conscious effort to put your knowledge into practice, you are less resistant to change because you are moving away from your "natural man" and toward your spiritual self. You are better able to deal with the paradoxes which will inevitably present themselves. Eventually you will "become" what you "know."

Now that I have admitted my inadequacy as a teacher and referred you to my superiors for a second opinion, I'd like to share some general ideas on dealing with youth burnout. But before I get back on my soap box and spew out a list of do's and don'ts I must acknowledge another weakness in parent education. In the pure sciences you can be pretty sure that if you follow a given formula the results will be predictable. When you deal with people you forfeit this guarantee.

Some parents say and do all the wrong things (in the gospel according to Day) and turn out happy, well-adjusted kids by the dozens. Others rear their children by the book, having used "I messages" and "feeling words" and "active listening" and "behavioral objectives," yet seem to have no end of trouble with their families. There are a couple of intangibles working here.

The first can be explained by the use of such abstract words as *spirits, vibes,* and *essence.* One mother, for example, can be so full of love that she can make a kick in the pants feel like a pat on the back. Another can be so full of masked hostility that she can say "I love you" and relay the message ". . . and if you believe that, I've got some swampland in Florida I'd like to sell you." Our kids would rather see a sermon than hear one any day, but it's the messages they *feel* that really make the difference. All the more argument for cultivating unconditional love as a life-style.

The second intangible is the child himself. Our belief in the premortal existence should make this fairly easy to understand. It's not as if we're blessed with a given number of globs

Kid Burnout: The Solution

of clay and allowed to shape them as we will. The spirit which comes to us in the body of a baby already has a form. It may be tough or fragile, resilient or rigid. One child may flourish under a certain form of discipline. while another might completely fold under the same conditions. I swear, there are some kids who would probably grow up healthy and happy in the worst of all possible homes, and others who seem to need more love and attention than two human parents are equipped to provide. How this relates to the premortal existence I'm not sure, but some types of emotional disturbances are thought to be inherited and to be caused more by the child's genetic makeup than by past experiences. Considering all these variables, anyone who sells a child-rearing philosophy with a money-back guarantee hasn't thoroughly researched his product.

Given all that, there are certain parental practices which encourage a susceptibility to burnout. The first, as I have hinted, is the practice of making threatening or judgmental statements about a child's behavior. "Jesus won't love you if you do that." "You're a bad girl." "I'm ashamed of you." Kids are going to make stupid mistakes, some of which may even qualify as sins. It's not your place to sentence your child to outer darkness before he even reaches the age of accountability!

Surprisingly, lavish praise can put a child in the position of slave if it's done in a calculated manner. When a parent gives generous praise for accomplishments and either punishes or ignores a child when he isn't accomplishing, he is saying to his child, "You only merit my attention when you achieve." Calculated praise and ignoring certainly have their places in the educational process—I admit that a lot of what I do with my students at school involves behavior modification. Still, a parent must constantly take care to show his child that his love is not given as a reward for good works. Spontaneous hugs, kisses, and frequent reminders that "I love you just because you're you" provide the basis for enduring self-esteem. And when you do share your child's joy at making an accomplishment, whether it's riding a bike without training wheels for the first time or earning a scholarship to Yale, remind him that one of the reasons you're so happy about it is that you know how good it makes him feel.

As for punishment, I think it's overrated. Research has shown that the use of positive consequences, or rewarding good behavior, is more effective than punishment. Of course we have to enforce limits, and when a child or youth does something that is wrong he must suffer the consequences, but I have seen some parents overstep their boundaries and become punishment-happy. Some parents actually appear to be vengeful in their child-rearing practices.

Punishment is especially not recommended in cases of kid burnout. By the time the child or youth begins showing the symptoms of anxiety or depression, he has had about as much negative stuff as he can handle. Further punishment is so painful it is often not even acknowledged. That's where adults get the idea that "he just doesn't care." "Nothing works." "He's a lost cause."

One popular punishment these days is "restriction." When a young person gets a poor grade, gets in late at night, talks back, or commits any rule infraction, he is temporarily banished from society as he knows it. Restriction can consist of anything from "Stay in your room for the rest of the night" to "You can't go anywhere except school and church for a month." While this is a great way to make an occasional impression on a happy and sociable kid, it's bad news for the burned-out youth. When a kid is depressed he suffers from feelings of isolation. He chooses to isolate himself from others, although that is the worst possible thing for him. When we isolate a burned-out kid we are depriving him of the very thing that will help him to regain a healthy zest for living—participation in wholesome activities with other people. If you have to restrict something, restrict the amount of time spent watching television.

At school I have the reputation of being a Darla Do-good, because I'm always trying to find ways of rewarding positive behavior rather than punishing unacceptable behavior. It's not because I'm softhearted or wishy-washy that I do this, it's

Kid Burnout: The Solution   77

because I've discovered that with discouraged kids, punishment just *doesn't* bring about the desired results. Most people fight this approach, arguing that the kid is doing all kinds of unacceptable things, and he doesn't *deserve* a reward. And they're probably right. It does seem a little unfair that Prudence Pratt, who has never even participated in a heated discussion during her five years in school, gets taken for granted, while Slugger Sloane gets a smiley-face sticker every time he goes five minutes without putting his fist in someone's teeth. The truth is, words like *fair* and *deserve* don't have a place in the remediation process. Let the Lord judge who's good and who's bad—our job is to help those who are down to get back on their feet. The idea that's important here is "they need love most when they deserve it least."

I've about decided that most of our problems stem from low self-esteem. As a parent, self-esteem is probably the most important thing you can give your child. You give it best by having it yourself; most learning is done by modeling. But along with having a good example a child needs to learn to appreciate his own uniqueness, and to know that his own self is worthwhile as a *self*, not only to the extent that he conforms to other people's ideas of what he should be.

It's difficult for me to talk to a group of kids about this concept, because when I say "be true to the self inside, and not the self that others want to make of you" it sounds as if I'm giving them permission to go against their parents' council. Yet this sense of loyalty to one's true self is the very core of self-esteem in teenagers. As parents we need to ask ourselves searchingly, "Which of the rules I set for my children are crucial to their growth in the gospel and which ones am I using to gratify my own ambition for them?" Then, having selected the teachings that are necessary for their eternal progress (and I include in this category dependability, good work habits, and the cultivation of the basic skills necessary to a successful life), we must ask whether we are teaching these skills the Lord's way, or in other words, by "persuasion, by long-suffering, by gentleness and meekness, and by love unfeigned; by kindness, and pure knowledge, which shall greatly enlarge the soul without hypocrisy, and without guile," and "reproving . . . with sharpness [only] when moved upon by the Holy Ghost." (D&C 121:41–43.)

As we teach our children the rules of conduct that are essential to their happinesss, we can also teach them the importance of getting in touch with their own unique, non-duplicatable, one-of-a-kind selves. We may have to make some compromises. So you always wanted to be a concert pianist and never had the opportunity, and now you can afford to give *your* child the chance you never had. Great, but be sensitive. There's a chance that your child sees Rachmani-noff as a poor substitute for Dale Murphy as a role model. Is that so bad? It will be extremely frustrating if you discover that your kid's mind functions in a manner that's completely foreign to you, but respect the difference. Different doesn't necessarily mean wrong. The more you can convince your child that you respect his right to his own ideas, the less he will need to try to convince you that he doesn't need your values.

Kids also need to know that they are respected. Some adults believe that they earned a right to be respected when they turned twenty-one, but that's not true. All of God's creations are entitled to respect—not just people, but plants and animals as well. Maybe plants and animals can function without it, I don't know. But people can't, regardless of their ages. It drives me nuts to hear an adult interrupt a child as if the kid weren't even there, or to discuss a child's problems and shortcomings right in front of him. We act like chickens, with a well-established pecking order. As if we deserve to push little people around just because *we* put in our time being pushed around and survived to adulthood. The cycle has to be inter-rupted if we want to teach our kids to respect themselves.

In addition to feeling that we are respected, all of us need the sense of power which comes from feeling that we are in control of our own lives. I talked earlier about the necessity of giving up this control in order to show obedience to the Lord. Yes, that's important, but when we do that it is our decision—we do it from our free agency because we know that as we unite our resources with those of our Father in Heaven our personal power is increased. We don't feel frustrated when we

Kid Burnout: The Solution

submit ourselves to the Lord, but we do feel frustrated when another human being usurps the control that rightly belongs to us.

Probably the single most baffling question facing parents involves control. We know we should always know where our kids are and what they are doing, and we know that we should set limits to keep our kids out of compromising situations. We know, too, that we must teach our children good habits and basic skills so they can be successful in life. A certain amount of involvement in the decision-making process is outlined in our job description. Still, when we step over the line and try to exert too much control we may find ourselves, and our kids, in trouble. Kids who feel stifled by an overabundance of parental control may assert their independence by rebellion, or they may become helpless. People who feel that they lack power to control their own lives often become depressed.

I've suggested ways that you can look at your own need to control your kids' lives, and I sincerely believe that after you've covered the areas of safety and morality (in a broad sense), the more room you can give your children to make their own decisions, the better. You can teach a child to control his own life by discussing with him the steps in the decision-making process, and giving him as much guidance as he wants as he solves his own problems. Even with a young child, you can help him much more by acting as a sounding board as he attempts to make his own decisions than by giving him the answer, all wrapped up and tied with a ribbon. Some of us don't even begin to learn the meaning of faith until we find it necessary to give our children the space they need to grow.

There comes a time in every person's life when he must discover that he is responsible for his own circumstances. Those of us who never learn this will, to some extent, remain emotional cripples. Kids need to know that their parents aren't perfect, and no matter how hard we try to teach and guide and set examples and fill needs, we are going to fail in some areas. No parent is completely adequate. They need to know that while we've always loved them and always will, we are still in the process of learning how to give perfect love, just as they are, and that we have made, and will continue to make, mistakes. We need to teach our kids that they have the power to change their own lives—through changing their actions, by changing their thinking, and by becoming acquainted with their spiritual, or inner, selves.

Kids also need to know that even when they make the wrong decisions, or fail to accomplish, or assert their independence, they are accepted. Two of the greatest fears known to man are the fear of rejection and the fear of loss of self. If our kids have to choose between being themselves and being accepted, they are in a no-win situation.

I recently heard a story about a young man who was in a situation where he had to work closely with another young man whom he found to be totally unacceptable. He tried to get transferred to another department, but this was impossible. He did everything he could to get the other young man to change his behavior, but with no luck. Finally, in desperation, he went to his Father in Heaven and prayed, "Please help me to see this man as you do." You can guess the results. As the first young man was blessed with the ability to see his co-worker through the eyes of the spirit, the relationship changed. The second young man's behavior changed. This is an example of unconditional love—the kind of love that will help us through the difficult times with the kids in our homes and in our priesthood and mutual classes.

Shall the Youth of Zion Flicker? 7

To Youth:

> You've been keeping to yourself these days
> Cause you're thinking everything's gone wrong
> Sometimes you just want to lay down and die
> That emotion can be so strong
> But hold on
> Till that old second wind comes along.
>
> Billy Joel[1]

Trivia Question: Who were Archie, Betty, Veronica, and Reggie?

Answer: They were a group of fictitious kids on the radio and in comic books in the fifties and sixties. They reappeared recently in cartoon form on their own television show. I started listening to "Archie" when I got too old for "Let's Pretend" and "The Buster Brown Show," and when it was too early in the day for "Your Hit Parade." That was when all the

---

1. "You're Only Human (Second Wind)," by Billy Joel. © 1985 Joel Songs. All rights administered by Blackwood Music, Inc. All rights reserved. International copyright secured. Used by permission.

situation comedies were on radio, and television was just a fantastic rumor. Archie and his gang were like the "Happy Days" kids but a little bit less believable.

I used to think that Archie and company were typical teen-agers. Their biggest problems were of this caliber (my plot): In order to make themselves look important one of the members of the gang suggested to the studentbody that they had sched-uled the famous singing group, Mickey and the Meatballs, to perform for the Senior Prom. A show evolved from the gang's magnificent maneuvering to get the Meatballs to cancel their world tour and sing at the prom. Although they never pre-tended it was easy, the gang always managed to save face in the end.

With kids like that as a standard, my life was pretty dull. For one thing, I would have been *thrilled* to have had a prob-lem like theirs, because it would mean that I had managed to get on the dance committee. For another, for most of my school career I felt quite isolated. It wasn't until high school that I had a group of friends I could even tentatively refer to as "the gang."

I was always Freda Fringe—not completely left out of things, but never securely in the middle of the action either. A few real highlights stand out, like the time my secret idol wrote "keep using that darling smile" in my yearbook, and the time my P.E. teacher chose me to be in a play and made me feel like a with-it and talented individual, something I obviously was unable to do for myself. I usually managed to get a date for the big school dances, but I never thought of myself as popular.

Like you, I had some really good times and some really horrible times. One of the horrible times took place during the summer of my senior year. When I was growing up, all the Salt Lake County communities had their own summer celebra-tion. We went to Union Fort Days on the Fourth of July, and to the Draper Parade on the Twenty-fourth. My community, Midvale, had Harvest Days later in the summer.

I'll never forget the day they came to my door—two of the guys I knew at school. They were soliciting candidates for Harvest Days Queen, and they wanted me to compete. Was I ever flattered! The truth is, we had to pay money to get in the

Shall the Youth of Zion Flicker? 83

running, and to these boys, I'm sure, it was purely a business proposition. But I took their suggestion that I run as a vote of confidence. My parents said that I could do it, and they bent over backwards to make it a great experience for me. My mother made me a gorgeous dress out of white polished cotton with red roses on it. I still remember that dress—it was one of my favorites. Then Mother took me out to shop for my first store-bought formal, complete with satin shoes dyed to match.

My parents were there in the audience the night of the pageant. I was more excited than afraid, and I thought I was beautiful. I even entertained thoughts of winning—if not queen, then maybe first or second attendant. I listened as my friends were introduced. Some were greeted by a polite trickle of applause, some by loud, enthusiastic cheers. Then it was my turn, and I guess I exhibited something short of a model's self-assurance as I walked across the stage. Forget the applause; forget the cheers. I heard them announce my name, and the next sound I heard was *laughter!* To this day I don't know what everyone was laughing at—whether my slip was showing, or whether my "darling smile" had gobs of spinach between its teeth, or whether I was just so obviously not the beauty queen type that my lack of polish inspired levity. I have no idea how I made it through the second stage of the competition, the evening dress modeling, or whether I even had the courage to get on the stage again. I only remember sitting with my parents after the finalists had been chosen, and hearing them assure me that I was wonderful. I still feel that sinking feeling of humiliation whenever I think about it. Maybe that's why I can't stand to watch the Miss Universe pageant on TV, and why I tell my daughters that beauty pageants are for "airheads."

I've lain awake nights trying to figure out a way to trick you into reading this chapter, because I think it's important. I spent an entire day dishing out pages of helpful advice and council, but the computer miraculously destroyed it. It must have been too preachy.

Since all else has failed, I've decided to be completely honest. The truth is, this is a chapter about the dark side of the teenage years, about the days and weeks that nothing goes right, and the times when you begin to wonder whatever possessed your premortal spirit to sign up for that long and difficult course, Life 101. The problem is, most people don't *like* to read about the bad news. We think that if we don't recognize the uncomfortable parts of life that they'll go away. Not long ago a stake Relief Society president asked me to come to a women's conference and talk about depression. But, she said, I'd have to think of a misleading title, because no one would *want* to go to a class about depression. It would be too depressing!

This chapter is for those of you who sometimes feel like I did after my ego was completely deflated by the queen contest incident, and for those of you who sometimes feel overwhelmed by all the pressures in your life. It's also for those of you who pretty much have it all together, and would be willing to do some peer counseling to help the kids in your ward or in your school who are in need of an understanding ear. And certainly it's for those of you who are bored, or discouraged, or despairing a lot of the time.

Probably kids between the ages of twelve and twenty do more emotional "work" than do people at any other stage of their lives. Aside from the fun—the friends, the parties, the telephone conversations, and the activities and sports—growing up is a *chore*. The business of the teenage years involves two big jobs: (1) Finding out who you are and establishing your own individuality, and (2) integrating your self into the group you see as important (society). Trying to perform these two tasks at once is like walking a tightrope. It is tempting as you try to become accepted by others (your friends, for example) to give up some of your self. And it is frustrating as others try to shape and mold you (your parents, for example), because you feel a desperate need not to allow your self to conform to someone else's pattern. When, for some reason or another, either your goal to be your own true self or your goal to be accepted by your own society is not realized, you are likely to experience a lot of turmoil and pain.

I use the term *kid burnout* to describe what happens when the turmoil and pain become so intense or last for so long that they give a kid a feeling of hopelessness. Burned-out kids don't

Shall the Youth of Zion Flicker?   85

get a lot of joy out of life. They feel bored most of the time. They spend a lot of time alone, either watching television or just "hanging around." They may feel as if they are isolated from other people, or they may need the security of being in the middle of a crowd, because it is uncomfortable to be alone. Burned-out kids hate school. They dread getting up in the morning. They find it hard to concentrate, and as a result they have trouble with their grades. Or they drive themselves unmercifully, because they are desperately afraid to come in second best. Burned-out kids have a long-term case of "the blahs."

Some people believe that when you attach a label like "burnout" to a condition, you are giving the condition respectability, as if to say, "As long as we have a name for it, it's okay to suffer from it—in fact, it's quite 'with it' to have the latest problem." These people are sure that just because I've given a name to that "nowhere," depressive feeling, half the population will decide they're burned out and pine away into oblivion. I don't believe that, because I don't believe anyone is stupid enough to suddenly develop pain or stagnation just because someone told them those conditions existed. What I'm hoping is that some of those great numbers of youth who *are* experiencing some pain and despair will understand what's happening and learn what to do about it, and that the others, those who love life and enjoy living, will reach out to help those who need a friend.

The most important thing to know is that you can change the way you feel. No one else can do it for you, no matter how much they love you or how much they want to help. One of the reasons people become depressed is that they feel that they are not in control of their own lives. The best way I know that we can become undepressed is to *get control* of our own lives.

I'd be a liar if I were to tell you that getting control of your life is easy, because it's not. The more discouraged you are, the more difficult it will be, and the longer it will take for you to get back in control. There'll be some times when you think you're not making any progress at all, and these times will be the times when you think it's not worth the effort. Then all of a sudden you'll realize that, hey, you *are* starting to feel better, and people *are* starting to stand up and take notice, and you *do* remember how it was before you got the grizzlies. And then you'll be furious. Why? Because it took you so long to get started.

The first thing to do when you feel as if the world has caved in on you is to find someone you can talk to. I don't mean talk about the Top Twenty or the baseball strike or the latest gossip, I mean talk about *you:* Your fears, your feelings, your beliefs, or your lack of them. It would be great if the person(s) you can talk to could be one or both of your parents, because, believe me, even though they may act as if you're Atilla the Hun or the Bride of Frankenstein at times, they are crazy about you, and they'd do anything they could to help.

But it may not be. Sometimes kids and parents find themselves so sturdily locked into a power struggle that, try as they might, communication gets garbled and strained, and what starts out to be a heart-to-heart ends up being a knock-down-drag-out. If the width of the generation gap in your family makes the Grand Canyon look like a crack in the pavement by comparison, you may need to find a good listener outside your home. Your mutual or priesthood advisor is probably just sitting around *wishing* you would open up to him, and your bishop is probably wondering right now how he can make your birthday interview more meaningful. An older brother or sister, an aunt or uncle, a grandparent, a neighbor, or a school counselor may be the key to a close and helping relationship.

Of course you won't jump in, feet first and eyes closed. I mean, you wouldn't just go up to Brother Bricker, your newly called priests quorum advisor, and dump it all out at his feet before you even knew the color of his eyes. (Unless, of course, you needed help in a *hurry,* and there was no one else, in which case it would be better to unload on the *mailman* rather than to try to be stoic and get no help at all.) When you find a potential confidant, check him out. Tell him a little more about yourself than he already knows. Does he seem really interested? Do the questions he asks make sense to you? How does he react when you reveal that you're not perfect? Shocked? Understanding? Do you go away from your conversation feeling better than you did when you came?

Shall the Youth of Zion Flicker? 87

I don't know what it is that we adults do to convince you kids that we are so perfect or so innocent that you can't tell us what's really happening inside your head. Chances are, whatever you're thinking or feeling is probably something we have either thought or felt at some time during our lives, or if not, we've probably heard it from somebody else, or at least seen it in the movies. Often, for example, kids who are burned out, or depressed, develop doubts about the Church. That's okay. You can't be excommunicated for questioning: I don't even think you can be excommunicated for not believing! Most of us have entertained doubts from time to time, and the guilt you may build up by sitting around feeling that there is something wrong with you is far more likely to drive you away from the Church than is a little healthy skepticism. Whether you've made an absolute idiot of yourself, as I did in the beauty queen contest, or failed a crucial exam, or even broken a commandment, the first step toward picking up the pieces is often confiding in a trusted friend.

I suggest an adult as a helper because kids your own age may not have the experience necessary to help you to see what's really going on with you. While it's best to have someone at least a few years older than you are, and someone who has the same values as you do, to listen to you and occasionally advise you, it's also very important to have at least one friend your own age to give you a sense of belonging.

Unfortunately, making friends does not come naturally to a burned-out kid. That's understandable. Usually when we are unhappy we're not a lot of fun to be around. We complain. We grumble. We are so anxious to get attention ourselves that we forget to go outside ourselves and show concern for the needs of others. Often we expect more from our friends than they are willing (or able) to give. I often hear remarks like this from burnout victims: "She's no fun." "He's boring." "They wouldn't be interested in me—I'm not popular."

If I could remove one word from the English language it would be *popular*. So who *is* popular? Look in your high school yearbook and see. I'll bet if you listed all the kids in your school who are indisputably popular you'd come up with about 10 percent of the studentbody. That leaves 90 percent who are "unpopular." They all need friends too, you know! "Popular" is ridiculously connected with certain stations in life. Cheerleader. Athlete. Studentbody officer. Beauty queen. Does that mean that those kids in your school who prefer math to muscle are jerks? To risk sounding like a parent (or an "older person") I must testify, and I'd bet my life on this: You don't have to look like a *Seventeen* cover girl to be fun.

If it's really hard for you to relate to other kids you may want to work on another area first and leave this one for last. But if you see a lack of friends as one of your biggest problems and you'd like to get on with the solution, start here. No one else can make friends for you—the most important thing is that you assume responsibility for doing it yourself.

This may sound strange, but it will be a lot easier for you to make friends with other people if you make friends with yourself first. You can be your own worst enemy or your own best friend, depending on how you feel about being you.

The "you" that lived with your Father in Heaven before coming to this earth was a happy, talented, well-adjusted person—I promise. No matter what a pitiful creature you may sometimes think you are now, that original you, bubbling over with love and joy and capability, is still within you, just waiting to be released. The things you don't like about yourself, such as that dumb loud laugh that you do when you're nervous, that overweight body that makes you self-conscious, or that painful shyness that keeps you from making friends are, strangely, parts of a "protective self" that you built up, either by trying to please those around you or by trying to protect yourself from emotional injury. You can get rid of the stumbling blocks to happiness (I call them SDBs, or self-defeating behaviors)[2], and the first step is to decide that you want to get to know your real, or spiritual, self.

Don't let that word *spiritual* throw you. Spiritual refers to anything that is good, *not* necessarily goody-goody. You miss out on a lot of excitement when you believe that you can't be spiritual unless you're dressed up in your Sunday clothes,

---

2. Johnathan Chamberlain introduced this term in his self-help course. *Eliminating a Self-Defeating Behavior* (Provo, Utah: Brigham Young University Press, 1976).

Shall the Youth of Zion Flicker?

sitting in church, or reading the scriptures. I like to think of spirituality as consisting of (1) a good relationship with your Father in Heaven and (2) a good relationship with other people. Inseparably interwoven with these two conditions is a good relationship with yourself.

James MacArthur[3] did a fantastic job of describing the true (spirit) self and the false (protective) self that we create with those cumbersome habits we pick up in our attempt to please others or protect ourselves. I'll paraphrase his example.

Imagine you and a group of friends are having a sleep-over party at someone's house. Right in the middle of the party the Brinks truck pulls up in the driveway and the driver comes to the door of the playroom. (Our playroom is a converted garage and has an outside door—we'll assume your friend's does, too.) The driver brings in this huge, gorgeous diamond —bigger than the Hope diamond, bigger than Liz Taylor's diamond—I mean, it is *huge.* And it is the most brilliant, dazzling piece of jewelry you have ever seen.

You and your friends are stunned. You are so busy "oohing" and "ahhing" over the diamond that you hardly notice when your friend's parents and her little brother come down and say something about a house hijacker. They lock the door and announce that all of you will have to stay in your friend's playroom for a long period of time, maybe even several years.

Then another truck pulls up in the driveway. It's the garbage truck. Just like the Brinks man, the garbage man (sanitation engineer, if you prefer) acts like he knows what he's doing, and he dumps a load of sleazy, slimy, smelly garbage in the middle of your friend's playroom. Right on top of the diamond. He says something about the need for an antiseptic garbage dump, and announces that he will be bringing a load of garbage every day or so. Gross! You try to escape, but the door is guarded.

Now, your attention is turned from the perfect diamond to the putrid garbage. It becomes a challenge to discover the right direction to face or the right depth to breathe in order to lessen

---

3. James D. MacArthur and Roger D. Coplen, *Developing a Healthy Self-Image* (Orem, Utah: Ensign Productions, 1980).

the effects of the pungent aroma. You look at garbage. You talk about garbage. You think about garbage. Your life is consumed by a pile of rancid refuse.

And what about the diamond? Before too many weeks go by, you and your friends have forgotten about it. It demands little attention. But *it's still there.* And because it's hard and tough and of extremely high quality, it's value hasn't lessened. It's still there, a beautiful, priceless, unique diamond, right there in the room, for anyone who cares to look underneath all the garbage and find it.

The diamond, as you may have guessed, is your true self, or your spirit as God created it. The garbage is the self-defeating behaviors, or the defenses we adopt to protect ourselves. These behaviors, or defenses, may have been perfectly appropriate when they originated, but they turned against us when we continued to use them. Some examples of these behaviors are:

> Depression
> Shyness
> Lying
> Psychosomatic illness
> Perfectionism
> Overconcern with appearance
> Ego trips
> Overeating
> Feelings of superiority
> Feelings of inferiority
> Extreme jealousy
> Inability to control temper
> An overconcern with sex
> Drinking
> "Doing" drugs

Of course, there are more. Basically, anything you do which keeps you from knowing and being your best self is a destructive defense, or a self-defeating behavior.

It might be interesting to look at your defenses, or SDBs, and try to discover what you are trying to protect yourself from. It will be hard for you to accept this at first (it was for

Shall the Youth of Zion Flicker?

me!), but because we would rather have negative attention than no attention at all we sometimes do some pretty nonproductive things—like get sick, act helpless, or have temper tantrums—to get attention. Some of us have decided that the only way to please the important adults in our lives is to be superachievers, and we think the world will cave in on us if we get a *B* or don't excel in everything we do. Others have had such a hard time pleasing anyone that we've given up on it, and we have a hard time succeeding at *anything.* Just about any hang-up you have can be traced back to a fear or an unmet need.

I have a hard time finding the reasons for some of the goofy things I do, and if you can't do it, it's okay—you can still get control of your life. But I had one success in this area that I'd like to share with you. A good question to ask whenever you're doing something that makes you unhappy or less successful than you might otherwise be is, "What's the payoff for (being depressed, being helpless, being fat, being superhuman, etc)?"

Several years ago I developed a bad backache. It really hurt, and it really cramped my style. It wasn't serious enough for me to miss work, but while I was at work I premeditated each move and I moaned and groaned a lot. As soon as I got home from work I went to bed with the heating pad.

It stayed on and on until it got ridiculous. I went to the doctor. I tried the chiropractor. I got a blessing, and the blessing said that I'd be healed according to my faith. That made me mad, because at that time I had quite a negative attitude and I knew I'd never be able to muster enough faith to be healed. Eventually I got really sick and tired of having a backache. I was afraid it would never go away, and I knew I had to do something.

Having tried every outside source of help I could think of I tried the last resort. I knew that lower back pain was sometimes a psychosomatic ailment, and I figured that since the doctor couldn't cure the pain, the chiropractor couldn't fix it, and even the Lord wasn't about to heal it without my help, I'd consider my role in the disaster. I asked myself (seriously!), What payoff was I getting from being a poor, pitiful, little painful wimp? I could hear myself, whenever someone asked me to take a responsibility or to do something: "Oh, I can't (whimper). I've got this horrible backache!"

The only payoff I could think of was that when I had my backache, I didn't have to do my church job. I had just been put in an auxiliary presidency, and I *hate* organizational responsibilities. Then I asked myself, "Now, really, which is worse? Having to go to a few meetings and make a few phone calls or prolonging this excruciating pain?" Anyone in his right mind would know the pain was worse, when it was brought out into the open like that, and I really didn't like the image of the poor little sick soul, so I decided I'd do my job and give up the pain. It worked. I started feeling better almost immediately.

If you'd rather not worry about the garbage (your defenses), and go straight for the diamond (your real self), that's okay. One of the easiest ways to get in touch with your real self is to ask some simple questions and insist on some honest answers. What do you really like to do? What do you want? What kind of clothes make you feel gorgeous (good looking)? (I don't mean what kind of clothes get approval from others.) Who brings out the best in you? Why?

It is also helpful to put your memory in gear. Remember your earliest happy memory. Remember a teacher who made you feel good about yourself. Remember a time you were praised by an adult. What was it for? Remember a time someone complimented you on your looks. What was different about you that day? Remember the last time you had the uncontrollable giggles. (Sorry, guys. What do you call it when a man or boy laughs to the point of helplessness?) Remember a time when you did a great job on something just because it felt good, whether anyone else noticed it or not. Remember a time that you did something for someone and didn't take credit for it. Remember how it felt.

Sometimes kids lose sight of their true selves because they're trying so hard to be what everyone says they should be that they forget who they really are, or who they really want to be. Adults—especially religious, God-fearing adults—feel so strongly the responsibility of teaching you kids the way back to your Father in Heaven that they may overdo it with

Shall the Youth of Zion Flicker? 93

the "should's," "got-to's," and "or else's." Sometimes we, as parents and leaders, use scare tactics and guilt trips because that's the only way we know to impress on you the importance of staying on the straight and narrow. And sometimes you get so burdened with the responsibility of being Saturday's Warriors, The Chosen Generation, and The Light of the World that you may wonder if you can really live up to all that's expected of you.

That's part of the challenge of being, as my kids like to remind me, "one of the more intelligent spirits that were saved for the latter-days." From the standpoint of this chapter, the challenge is not so much that you have to live up to your potential as it is that you have to learn to deal with all the pressures we place on you. The truth is, it doesn't matter whether you're the only Mormon in your school, or whether you're on the stake youth committee, or whether you're the mission president's son, you're still a kid, and there's no way you could have reached perfection by now. I know you're reminded frequently that the salvation of your whole community may depend on the example you set (and it may!), but the real name of the game is "endure to the end," and the enduring will be a lot easier if you can give yourself a little moral support.

By suggesting that you don't have to be perfect I'm certainly not implying that you should go out and do something that you know is wrong. The commandments, the Word of Wisdom, and latter-day revelation are very basic guidelines, and they were given to us to protect our peace of mind, not to threaten it. But I am saying that you will be much happier and much more able to cope with the pressures that you will have to face if you can do the things you do because you know they'll get you where you want to go and not because you feel you're always having to prove yourself to someone. If, every once in a while, you show your humanness by getting a low grade or having to say no to a request for help, you're not setting a bad example. The best way to set a good example is to show people that you can be a mistake-making human being and live through it!

It's really important that you learn to love yourself. I don't mean that you should act as if you know you're great, or admire your looks in the mirror every time you get a chance.

When you really love yourself you love others, too, and you don't have to show off or brag in order to prove your worth. When you love yourself you see yourself as no better or no worse than anyone else. You know that you are a child of God, and so is everyone else. When you have a true sense of your own self-worth you are able to enjoy your successes and forgive yourself for your failures.

It's a life's work to learn everything there is to know about loving and forgiving, and if I were to imply that you had to learn it all now, I'd be putting you on a guilt trip. The message I want to get across is not that you have to love and forgive because the scriptures say you do, but that life is so much easier and more pleasant if you develop love and forgiveness that it's worth a try.

Your parents need forgiving, too. Not for their own good, necessarily, but for yours. All kids get disillusioned by their parents at some time during their growing up years. Why? Because kids grow up thinking their parents are perfect. It's easy to be perfect to a little baby—you just have to pick him up when he cries and feed him when he's hungry. And it's not too hard to appear perfect to a little kid, as you tower above him and hand down edicts with wisdom and authority. But it's impossible to appear perfect to a teenage kid, one who's forming his own ideas about what life is and what a person should be. Even great parents have faults, and it's hard to hide them from someone who lives in the same house as you do.

Parents appear even less perfect when their imperfections affect their kids. For example, they're not always fair. If they always want to know where you are they're too strict. If they don't, they don't care. I remember when I was in high school. One of my friends was embarrassed because her mother was too old; another was embarrassed because hers was always pregnant. One hated being an only child—another hated being lost in the shuffle of a big family. Sometimes well-meaning parents can actually cause problems for their kids because they put too much pressure on them. Some parents try too hard; others seem not to try hard enough. But with all their trials and errors, I've never met a parent who got up in the morning and said to himself, "Today I'm going to do my best to make my kid's life miserable."

Shall the Youth of Zion Flicker?

So now you're no longer a hero-worshiping little kid, and you know the truth. Your parents are just people who have some good points and some bad, some talents and some hang-ups. They probably do the best they can, and to a kid who grew up expecting perfection, the best is never good enough. If you insist on staying the little kid and can't forgive your parents for their imperfections, you'll never accept responsibility for yourself, and you'll never get control of your own life. If your parents are overbearing, embarrassing, or seemingly uncaring, accept the fact. Let them be who they are. Then you can get on with being who you are.

Easy for me to say. I know. You still live in your parents' home, and they still have a lot of power over you. Some things you'll never change, like the way your parents refuse to let you stay out until the wee hours or the way they insist that you go to church on Sunday. Some things are negotiable, and you can put yourself in a better position to negotiate by learning a few simple rules of human relations. And there are other things, like your parents' personalities or the way they can make you feel like a total failure sometimes, that you can't change but you can learn to withstand.

Someone once said, "No one can make you feel inferior without your permission." It's true, but you have to learn how to withhold your permission. I think of the story of the paper boy who was known for his pleasant disposition. He always smiled and said "good morning" to everyone who passed by, whether they bought a paper or not. One day he was confronted by a real grouch, who, because the boy miscounted his change, went into a rage and made a lot of ungrounded accusations and shouted obscenities. It was a bad scene. As the man walked away, still muttering insults, the boy smiled and said, "Have a good day." A bystander, astounded at the boy's response, asked incredulously, "Why are you so nice to that old sorehead? He doesn't deserve a smile!" The boy answered, "Maybe not, but why should I let him control the way I feel? I enjoy being happy. Should I spoil my day just because some other guy is in a rotten mood?"

That boy was in control of his own life. You can be, too. You can't stop people from giving you put-downs, but you can stop yourself from being put down. When someone says (or more likely implies, by a snide remark, a dirty look, or a deadly silence) that you're stupid, you're lazy, or whatever, just think to yourself, "Well, you're entitled to your opinion," and remind yourself that basically you're a pretty good kid and that you're doing the best you can. If they give a direct criticism, ask yourself if there is anything you can gain from the criticism. Sometimes, if you're a big enough person, you can turn criticism into suggestion, and pick up an idea of how to improve yourself. But refuse to take criticism as a put-down.

Most of our problems revolve around the word *should*. Not only do we drive ourselves nuts, thinking *I should always be the best at everything*, or *I should be better looking than I am*, but we really make life difficult for ourselves by thinking other people should be different than they are. You could labor all the days of your life and probably you could never change your parents, or your teachers, or your friends. Who said other people should be kind and considerate and easy to get along with? The truth is, people are going to be the way they are going to be, and expecting them to be something they're not will only bring disillusionment. I really believe that the admonition to "judge not that you be not judged" is the real key to getting it all together. Life is so *simple* when you learn to allow others to be inadequate!

That sort of brings us back to the subject of friends.

Many of the things I have to say about making friends might be a little hard to swallow. They might go against your social code. Unfortunately, there's something about being your age that makes you want to defy the laws of friendability. Believe me, I understand, because it's always been that way. I can remember the unwritten laws that dominated the halls of Jordan High back in the dark ages (even before Elvis or the Beatles), and a quick survey of the scene today shows me that they haven't really changed. For example, "open" and "outgoing" is not cool. Even the word *cool* connotes aloofness. But look at the people you know, even those your own age, who are really happy. Somehow they manage to transcend *cool* and radiate warmth, ever so subtly.

Shall the Youth of Zion Flicker?

I'd be lying if I said that looks didn't have something to do with being liked. The way you look provides a first impression, and if the first impression isn't good, society doesn't always provide a second chance. I don't mean that you have to have been blessed with faultless features. I do mean to suggest that you do the most you can with what you have.

The old standby, cleanliness, is still most important. Nothing says "I don't care about myself, and you probably wouldn't like me either" like greasy hair, body odor, or bad breath. There's nothing mysterious about it, people are just more comfortable around other people who look and smell good. At least for this life, our bodies and our spirits are inseparably joined together, and if you like yourself it will show in the way you dress and the way you wear your hair.

Next to cleanliness, I think the most important thing about your dress and hair is that they are *you*. Usually we know instinctively what makes us look good and what makes us look ridiculous. I have a round face and thin, straggly hair, so, although I need a change every now and again, I always come back to a really short haircut with lots of fullness on top. Bright colors really turn on the lights in my face, and casual styles make me feel comfortable. A friend of mine looks absolutely elegant in tailored grays and browns, but the clothes that make her look classy would make me just disappear into the woodwork. Girls, get your colors analyzed—it will surprise you to see that the colors that fall into your "season" are the ones that you are naturally drawn to. Guys, you might find it fun to get yours analyzed too (if your dad will let you!). Men's styles are really getting colorful. If you think a color consultation is too feminine, just trust your instincts. Choose clothes that show off the real you.

Do the things that will let the spiritual you come through. If I could suggest only one thing to help you look better, feel better, and *be* better, it would be regular aerobic exercise. Aerobic exercise is any kind of exercise that stimulates your heart and lungs for a sustained period of time: running, walking, biking, jumping rope, swimming, and so on. Any exercise is better than none—a mile or two miles a day would help, although you will get maximum benefit if you exercise for an hour a day. You will be amazed at the things that happen to your face and your body when you exercise. Your complexion will not only clear up, it will *glow!* Your legs will look good; your body will assume its right proportions. Your appetite will normalize—you'll start craving healthy foods instead of junk food. But better than that, you'll feel great! It's almost impossible to be depressed when your body is in shape.

I'm convinced that my spirit is gorgeous. Comparatively, I mean. I don't expect to look like a movie queen when I'm resurrected, but I do expect to look as good as I've ever looked. I believe that my spirit is beautiful (looking) for several reasons.

One: Sometimes, when I have really let myself go, or when I am going through a really tough time emotionally or spiritually, I will look in a mirror and I won't even recognize myself. I believe that the reason I don't recognize myself is that the me I've grown to know and love is the me that looks like my spirit. When, because of too much stress and strain or too little tender loving care, I've strayed too far from that look, the face I see in the mirror is the false self I talked about earlier, and bears no resemblance to the real me.

Two: I believe that when I am really in tune spiritually, it is my spirit self that people see. I don't mean to make it sound spooky, like I turn into a ghost; I guess I mean that my spirit radiates through my body and sort of turns me "on." Let me give you a couple of examples.

Fasting isn't easy for me. I'll be honest. I only fast when it's absolutely necessary, like on fast day (and sometimes I even have trouble with that!), or when I'm in desperate need of spiritual guidance and all else has failed, or when I have to give a talk or a lesson and I really need some extra help.

Several years ago I was called to be a spiritual living teacher in Relief Society, and when the bishop set me apart he told me to fast before each lesson, so I did. During one lesson I particularly felt the Spirit. After the lesson one of the young women in the ward came up, with tears in her eyes, and said that the lesson had been a really spiritual experience for her. She said, "I kept looking up at you, and you *looked so pretty,*

Shall the Youth of Zion Flicker?

it just made me cry!" A second time, I had just moved to a new community, and I was called as in-service leader in the Primary. The first lesson I had to give, was, I felt, a really special one, and I wanted to give it all I had, so I knew I would have to study hard and fast and pray. I did so, and I felt good about the lesson. I became close friends with one of the women in the group, and she told me later that she had wanted to get to know me because of the way I had given the lesson that night. She said, "You looked *so beautiful!*"

People *never* tell me that I'm beautiful. They may say I'm a good teacher, or funny, or that I have eye-to-eye contact, but I'll bet I can count on one hand (well, maybe two) the number of times someone has commented on my good looks. It seems strange that two of these times (and you can bet I remember every one of them) were times when I really hadn't paid any extra attention to my looks, but when I had paid a lot of attention to my spiritual state. I guess the reason that I stress so strongly the need to get to know the real you is that these, and other experiences, have shown me that the real me is far better looking, more fun, and more loveable than any self that I could create. I'm sure you'll find the same about yourself.

While the way you look can have some effect on the first impression you make, the most important thing you can do if you want to have friends is to show people you care about them. I know, that sounds like a church lesson or a parent's preachment. I wish there were a way I could word it so it didn't sound trite, but the trouble is, it's true. If you could just get in the habit of showing an interest in everyone—listening when they talk, congratulating them on achievements, sending a birthday card, offering to bring work home when they're sick, the world would beat a path to your door.

I'm not saying that you should take the "puppy dog" approach. The puppy dog approach is when you sort of hero-worship someone and you are always hanging around them, complimenting them, doing things for them, letting them walk all over you. If you are launching an all-out campaign to make friends you could possibly overdo it if you showered all your attention on one person. That's why I suggest that you show an interest in everyone. You will always be interacting with people on several different levels. There will be people you really admire, who you know could be a good influence on you, and you'd like to get to know them better. Then there will be people who really need your help, who you are pretty sure you wouldn't like to spend all your time with, but you can certainly give them a few minutes a day. You never know, at the beginning, who will turn out to be a real, lasting friend. Getting in the habit of being helpful to everyone will help you to be open to that true friend when he or she comes along.

We've talked about some ways to cope with the ordinary, everyday problems of growing up. They are always with us. Unfortunately, some of you have had to, or will have to, deal with problems of much greater proportions during your teen-age years. The death of a parent, a serious illness (yourself or a member of your family), divorcing parents, even a move to a different part of the country can play havoc with your emotions. You may feel that you've been abandoned, either by someone you love or by your Father in Heaven. You may feel completely devastated, and completely alone.

If you are ever in a situation which really threatens the groundwork of your life—your hope, your testimony, even your will to live—please remember the suggestions I've made in this chapter. First, don't try to handle it alone. Of course, your Father in Heaven will help you, but you also need another human being to be close to. Give someone a chance. The hopelessness will pass if you can own your feelings, talk about them, and then, after a reasonable time, let them go. Second, you will be tempted to believe that because something so awful has happened to you, you really *don't* have control of your own life. While it's true that some things are beyond your control, you can still decide how you react to them. Just keep on keeping on.

> [and] Don't forget your second wind,
> Sooner or later you'll feel that momentum kick in.[4]

---

4. "You're Only Human (Second Wind)," by Billy Joel. © 1985 Joel Songs. All rights administered by Blackwood Music, Inc. All rights reserved. International copyright secured. Used by permission.

The Enlightened Mind

8

I've discovered the missing link.

I found it, of all places, in a staff development meeting. There I sat, leaning back in my chair with the movable desk-top, my legs stretched out, feet crossed. On the desk top sat my yellow legal pad, decorated with a few unexplainable doodles. I always brought a notebook to staff development meetings, but except for those times when we were inundated with instructions of a life-or-death nature (like how to fill out this year's federal forms) I seldom took notes. If I did take notes they were likely to be of ideas that popped into my head while the speaker was speaking. I always figured that anything worth remembering would be memorable enough that I wouldn't have to write it down.

This speaker was an important-sounding Yankee Ph.D. from Connecticut. He showed promise: he was funny. His subject was "Mind Styles."[1] Sounded a little heavy, but there was always hope. My eyes scanned the audience. I noticed a woman I thought I recognized, but I couldn't get her attention.

---

1. The concept of mind-styles is discussed in Anthony F. Gregorc, Ph.D., *An Adult's Guide to Style* (Maynard, Maryland: Gabriel Systems, Inc.).

I contemplated writing a letter to my mother. Surely she'd rather have a letter on legal pad paper today than one on real stationery next week. I stopped short. The speaker was doing a flawless job of describing *me!*

"I can tell you Abstract Randoms," he claimed, "by your note-taking behavior. Look at you. Sitting back in your chairs, your legs stretched out in front of you, crossed at the ankles. You all brought paper—you always do—but you never take notes, and if you do, they will more likely be of some idea that pops into your head, triggered by something I say, than of something I actually say. I'm on to you. You think that anything I say that's worth remembering will be so memorable that you won't *need* to write it down!" His clairvoyance stopped there. Thank goodness! He didn't mention the letter to my mother.

By the time I'd focused my mind and straightened up in my chair the speaker was talking about another group of people, a group he called the Concrete Sequentials. The Concrete Sequentials' note-taking habits, he said, were impeccable. They were constantly processing all incoming information, writing everything in outline form. I looked at the woman next to me. In a neat little notebook she had outlined everything that had been said so far, including the jokes, and she seemed to be agonizing over whether to treat the speaker's last remark as a subheading or to start with a new roman numeral. She was dressed more like an IBM executive than like my idea of a frazzled teacher, wearing a charcoal gray suit with a maroon tie at her throat. The tie was done up in a perfect bow. She wore high heels and hose, and her nails were polished and flawless. They matched her tie. I slumped in my chair, feeling suddenly tacky in *my* teaching uniform—bright blue-green cotton pants with a striped shirt, open at the neck and tied loosely at the waist. I arranged my feet beneath my chair in an attempt to hide the chipped toenail polish revealed by my open-toed sandals.

What I learned at that meeting possibly had more impact on my relationships with other people, and with myself, than anything I have ever heard. It all came together for me then:

The Enlightened Mind   103

forgiveness, self-acceptance, and unconditional love. I'd
always known I was supposed to accept other people as they
were, and I'd been trying to sell the idea for years. But until
that lecture I'd been so angry with, and so threatened by,
people like the woman sitting next to me in the gray flannel
suit that I'd never really been able to come to peace with
myself and my surroundings.

With Dr. Gregorc's permission, I'll make it as simple as
possible. While all of us have certain qualities in common, we
all are unique, and the sum of our individual qualities makes
us different from anyone else. While he has no intention of
trying to categorize human beings into neat little packages,
Gregorc has studied qualities of the mind, or mediation abilities, with special attention to two qualities: perception and
ordering. He has discovered that there are four dominant style
characteristics. He calls them Concrete Sequential, Abstract
Sequential, Abstract Random, and Concrete Random.

While it is possible for a person to be equally strong in each
of these four areas, most of us are stronger in one than in the
other three. There is no "good" or "bad" or "right" or "wrong."
Those who are equally strong in each area are not better
people than those who lean heavily toward a certain style,
although they may find life a little simpler. It is not better to be
predominantly one way or another, although each of us probably thinks our mind-style is the best.

The Abstract Random is the person (maybe because I am
one) I like to think of as the creative thinker. He is very people
oriented, and is very much tuned in to emotions and spirituality. He trusts his "inner guidance system"[2] and therefore
doesn't need a lot of external proof when he's making a decision or a judgement. Relationships are very important to the
Abstract Random, but along with needing other people he
needs some time alone "in the quiet of his psyche."[3] He doesn't
like rules and regulations, cold or unemotional people, or

---

2. Anthony Gregorc, Ph.D., *Style Delineator* (Maynard, Maryland: Gabriel
Systems, Inc.).

3. Anthony F. Gregorc, *An Adult's Guide to Style*, op. cit., p. 31.

routine procedures. He is comfortable hanging loose and going with the flow. He might be described as "flaky" or "off the wall."

The Concrete Sequential is seen as proper, well organized, practical, and conservative. He has very high standards for himself and for others, and in his attempt to "help" his family and co-workers to measure up to these standards, he may appear to be dictatorial. He is strong and stable and cool, calm, and collected; responsible, patient, and hardworking; punctual, dependable, and impeccable. An unsanitary, unordered environment can drive the Concrete Sequential up the wall.

The individual whose dominant mind-style is Abstract Sequential may be described loosely as "intellectual." He is very logical, and bases his judgments on scientific evidence. He is able to detach himself from the issue he is examining and to research and weigh values and facts carefully. He needs an environment that is mentally stimulating and he enjoys sharing his ideas with others who share his interests and abilities. He is impatient with sentimentality or illogical ideas. If the whereabouts of the lost ten tribes is ever discovered through a scientific search, we will almost certainly have an Abstract Sequential to thank for it.

If the Abstract Random is a creative thinker, then we might call the Concrete Random a creative "doer." Concrete Randoms make great mini-class chairpersons—it was undoubtedly a CR who invented glass grapes and net tub scrubbers. Like the AR, the Concrete Random's thinking process emphasizes intuition and instinct, independence and insight. He is described as original and unique. CRs are often "born leaders" and great competitors. They dislike hard and fast rules and bland surroundings.

Dr. Gregorc's study of mind-styles was carried out primarily to help improve communication between teachers and students. You can imagine the implications an understanding of mind-styles could have on education. Picture, for example, the Concrete Sequential teacher (and many teachers *are* Concrete Sequential) trying to teach an Abstract Random kid. She's sure that the kid either has a learning disability or he's

The Enlightened Mind 105

just plain crazy, and his messy desk and unconventional
answers will drive her bonkers. Without an understanding of
mind-styles the teacher will undoubtedly make this child's life
as miserable as he makes hers.

Or, picture the Abstract Sequential, whose mission it is to
enlighten the seeking minds of the future Jonas Salks and Leo
Tolstoys of the world. How can he hope to relate to those
students who see science and literature simply as a necessary
ten credits on the road to the really *important* things, like
taking over the insurance business? And how can the Concrete
Sequential child relate to the Abstract Random teacher who
repeatedly says "We'll do that tomorrow" on a Friday?

Believe me, this idea has great potential for helping
teachers relate to kids, for helping kids to tolerate teachers,
and for helping teachers to get along with each other. There's
no doubt in my mind that that Gregorc lecture was the turning
point between my fight with "The System" and my conviction
that I still belonged in the teaching profession. I'd realized
years earlier that somewhere between the radiant coed I'd been
and the burned-out teacher-wife-mother-drudge I'd become,
I'd lost the thing I needed most, my self-esteem. Although I'd
rather have been tortured than have admitted it, I'd allowed
myself to think (no, thinking is a conscious act—this was just
something I'd assimilated), well, to believe, that because I
wasn't like the faultlessly put-together woman in the gray suit
and maroon tie, who'd undoubtedly left her beds made and
her breakfast dishes washed, I'd missed the boat somewhere.
And because others like her, especially when they were in
positions of authority over me, made me feel like such a dip
stick, I had to manufacture reasons to hate them (it wasn't
hard) in a frantic attempt to like myself.

If understanding each other's mind-styles helps teachers
and students, just think what an impact it could have on relationships between employers and employees, husbands and
wives, parents and children, or sisters and brothers! Especially
given the fact that for some bizarre reason a great many of us
marry people whose thinking is as opposite from ours as is
humanly possible. We could lay to rest the lament, "we have
nothing in common" forever, simply by accepting the fact that

it's true, you and your wife or husband may *not* be alike, but it's not because your spouse doesn't care enough about you to develop interests similar to yours, it's just that his or her mind is put together so differently from yours that he or she may not even be able to perceive your interests as potentially interesting!

Each mind-style has its own particular traits which can make its possessor next to impossible to live with. Abstract Randoms are likely to be chronic latecomers. Their housekeeping skills may leave something to be desired. They tend to be self-centered, moody, jealous, overdependent, and extravagant. They worry too much. Concrete Randoms are known for their tendency to start something without finishing it or to forget promises or agreements. They have no patience with people who don't possess their intuitive gifts. They may be more concerned with a pet project than with the rights of those around them.

Abstract Sequentials have no tolerance for people who don't think like they do. They may be absent minded. They can be harshly critical, and if you don't measure up to their idea of intellectual excellence they can make you look stupid by using two-bit words and sounding like a summit-level symposium right there at your dinner table. They savor solitude.

Inflexible and *rigid* are words often used to describe the Concrete Sequential. He may be extremely critical, and at the same time be excessibely defensive at receiving criticism. He likes to control things *and* people. It's next to impossible to engage a CS in an intellectual or philosophical discussion, so don't try. Sympathy and compassion do not come naturally to the Concrete Sequential.

As you can see, any combination of any two mind-styles could be disastrous. The old saying that "opposites attract" is usually true. There seems to be some unexplainable chemistry between direct opposites, such as Concrete Sequentials and Abstract Randoms, which brings them together in a commitment to eternal togetherness which is guaranteed to make Jason's quest for the golden fleece a mean task by comparison. Acceptance of the idea that different is not synonomous with wrong is a giant step in the direction of unconditional love, not just for others but for yourself as well.

The Enlightened Mind 107

Let's review some of the reasons for burnout I outlined in chapter 2:

1. Being guided by a driving force rather than a rational plan.
2. Being guided from without, rather than from within.
3. Expectations which are out of line with reality.
4. The belief that we can't make a difference.

A working understanding of mind-styles can do a great deal to annihilate these four conditions. The first reason, being guided by a driving force, is indirectly related to mind-styles, but it is related. We become compulsive when we lose sight of our authentic selves, and often we desert our true selves in our attempt to please someone else. When we understand and accept the concept that mind-styles are very personal but also completely respectable, and when we understand that sometimes the negative feedback we get from others is not so much because *we* don't measure up as because the accusor needs to criticize, it becomes easier for us to be who we are, and the use of defense mechanisms becomes less important to our emotional survival.

Finding out who we are, and acting accordingly, is our life's work. For me, anyway, the more I came to understand the meaning of mind-styles in my life the easier it was for me to understand what and who I was and to give myself permission to be that person. I was able to look at my gifts more appreciatively and my shortcomings more objectively. It didn't give me permission to rationalize my weaknesses, and *keep* them, but it did help me to understand, for example, why it takes me all day to do a job that a Concrete Sequential can do in an hour.

Abstract Randoms like me are *supposed* to be late and disorganized. As I've grown older (or maybe as I've grown *up*), however, I've discovered that my lateness and disorganization have been the root of many of my problems. It's to my advantage, therefore, to look at my innate characteristics and decide which ones I want to keep and which ones I want to modify. *It's my decision.*

I love being perceptive, tuned in, and instinctive. My ability to establish rapport with others has served me well. The knowledge that I can evoke tears or laughter by putting words together on a printed page sends me into orbit. I treasure the inordinate number of hours I've spent rummaging through Peachtree Salvage[4] for just the right gag gift, and the nights I've stayed up because the inspiration to give a homemade gift came inconveniently late.

I may *act* like an airhead, but I'm not *stupid*. I've learned that in order to survive at work I have to write behavioral objectives, submit my reports before the deadline, and get to school on time. The adjustment has been painful, but I'm getting good at it. I've learned that at home, as exciting as it may be to make as big a mess as I can and then fly into a frenzy an hour before the white-gloved company comes, living that way takes more energy than I've got. And while my extreme sensitivity gives me a remarkably high EQ[5], it doesn't do much for my mental health. I'd like to stay sensitive to others' feelings while I toughen up my own.

Knowing my inherent strengths and weaknesses gives me a starting point toward perfection. I don't mind the effort it takes to overcome my undesirable characteristics, because it's my idea now. When I was changing myself to conform to the whims of the nearest Concrete Sequential, or to impress a significant Abstract Sequential, I was dying spiritually. My enhancing qualities were going down the drain along with the inconvenient ones. When I was lashing out in defiance against the rule-maker and the nix-sayers I was sick with anger. Needless to say, I was hurting myself more than I was hurting them (whoever *they* are, or were.) Now, I no longer feel guilty for not living up to someone else's ideal, for having the nerve to be who I am. I feel a silly sense of pride at my reputation as the School Kook, but knowing the limitations of my position I won't jeopardize my safety. I will never go to pink hair or purple leg-warmers.

Can you see, too, how understanding mind-styles can help us to keep our expectations in line with reality? I can't count how many times I've been disillusioned because I *assumed* some one would feel, or act, a certain way, and was devas-

---

4. The local junk store.
5. Empathy Quotient.

The Enlightened Mind

tated when they didn't. As many times as I've had my expectations shattered I still do it. I assume that because someone is nice, or has a neat sense of humor, or is from my hometown, they *think* like I do. I expect them to agree with my ideas, appreciate my work, and share my innermost thoughts.

It very seldom happens that way. I can count on one hand the number of friends I've had who really think like I do. I can remember one in particular. We used to work on committees together (usually committees of two, because no one else wanted to work with us), and our thought processes were so similar it was eerie. We used to interrupt each other all the time. It was a compliment to be interrupted—what we really did was finish each other's sentences. She would start to say something, and I would get on her wave length, and I'd get so excited I'd have to shout it out. Neither of us was ever insulted by the interruption, because it was an affirmation of our own vision. She'd say, "Hey, we could . . . ," and I'd say, "Yes, and then we'll . . ." The final product was almost always fantastic, but never as exciting as the process.

Friends like that are rare. My mistake was believing that a friend had to be someone who thought like I did, who felt the same way I did, and who could practically read my mind. Not until I revised my expectations did I realize that I could cultivate a deep and lasting friendship with someone who had as little comprehension of my inner workings as I did of his, but who cared enough to like me anyway.

The fourth cause of burnout is the belief that we can't make a difference. Where working (or living) with people with opposing mind-styles is concerned, the best way to fight burnout may well be to admit that in some areas, such as changing someone else's basic personality, we can't, and shouldn't try to, make a difference. Deep down inside, each of us loves his own package of character traits, and we'll resist like crazy when anyone tries to change them.

The second best way to fight burnout (or tied for first) is to make a difference in ourselves by knowing who we are and by capitalizing on what we know. There's no limit to what we can become, but before we become anything worthwhile we must learn to love ourselves as we are. When we love ourselves as we are, we can love others as they are. It all boils down to that, doesn't it? Love radiates warmth. Acceptance fosters love. Maybe what we need is not more understanding, but more compassion for those who we will never understand, and more forgiveness for ourselves and our inability to ever completely comprehend what makes our fellow workers, mates, parents, or children tick.

How to Prevent Being the Burner

9

The Golden Rule has a nice ring to it, but it has some limitations. When we do unto others as we would have them do unto us, we assume that others have the same wants and needs as we do, and that's not always true.

When my kids were little I started a nursery school in my house. The school grew, and my dog chewed up my expensive materials, so I moved to a building. I added more classes and employed other teachers, and found myself in the position of director. I dealt with my "faculty" the way I have always wanted to be dealt with. I gave them a few basic guidelines (Don't beat the children, put in an honest day's work, and do your best to foster a warm, creative learning environment) and left them alone. I thrive on freedom. Doesn't everybody? Not necessarily.

What I discovered was that one of my teachers, the one that was most like me, took the ball and ran with it. She did a great job, and she loved working there. Some others liked working there too, but they did the bare minimum (they came). I felt betrayed. How could anyone fail to flourish under such an environment? They had small classes, the best materials, and, you guessed it, a warm and creative working environment. Still others were extremely conscientious and did a great job, but, I discovered, they were extremely frustrated. They were always asking, "What am I supposed to be doing [in this situation]?" They were never satisfied with my (I thought facilitative) answer, "I trust your judgment. Do what you think is best."

What I discovered from that experience, and what further experience and research has reinforced, is that not everyone works well with a lot of freedom. Some people need close supervision to guarantee that they will work at all; others feel more comfortable with a lot of structure. The old saying "One man's meat is another man's poison" certainly holds true where motivation is concerned.

My supervisory behavior is an exception to the rule. Most administrators lean toward the concrete sequential mind-style and are likely to assume, therefore, that because *they* function better with a lot of structure and a minimum of ambiguity, everyone does. Just as it was beyond my realm to understand why an intelligent, capable person would *want* to be given a step-by-step plan of action, these leaders find it impossible to believe that someone (and especially someone on a lower rung of the ladder than they) can function without constant pushing and reminding. While I looked on my nonautonomous employees as helpless, the concrete-sequential administrator undoubtedly looks on people with a strong need for self-direction as difficult. Until all of us realize that what motivates one person may threaten another, we are potential contributors to job/church job/kid/student/marriage/missionary burnout.

It's true that the burnout victim himself is responsible for his own rehabilitation. By including a chapter on enlightened leadership I am by no means saying that you are responsible for your employee's/mate's/kid's/student's state of mind, but let's face it. Whether you look at it from a spiritual standpoint (aren't you your brother's keeper?) or from a purely practical point of view (burned-out staff members aren't going to bring your percentages up, whether you're concerned with sales, production, or home teaching), it's to your advantage to run your organization (and an organization can be anything from a family to a corporation) in a manner that will foster illumination and ignition as opposed to immobility.

How to Prevent Being the Burner　　　　　　　　　　　*113*

Just as we learn our parenting practices by observation, many of us learn our leadership methods by modeling. Oh, sure, we go to seminars and staff development sessions, and sometimes we even try a new idea to see whether it will work, but most of us have a preconceived picture of what a "boss" does, one that began forming in our minds when we were children. And unless we are either extremely open minded or glaringly unsuccessful in our role the way we have learned it, we go on following the path of least resistance, leading the way we were led.

When I was a young adult I almost always had a calling in the youth organization, and it usually involved dramatics. I had a pretty good relationship with the youth, and we were usually well satisfied with the plays and roadshows that evolved from our labors. I can remember one particular time, though, when I found that my usual casual approach wasn't getting the results I wanted. You can picture the situation. Performance time was drawing near, and the cast was nowhere near ready. Kids were missing practices and goofing around and just not living up to my expectations. I attributed our lack of progress to cast apathy.

I'd never taken a class or even read a book on directing. I probably hadn't even perused what was then the *Drama Director's Manual*, so all I knew about being a director was what I'd seen in the movies and observed from my high school drama teacher. I'd learned one thing: All the *great* directors were extremely temperamental; they yelled a lot. Then, I guessed, the trouble with my cast was that I'd been too even-tempered. If it was yelling they needed, I vowed, it was yelling they'd get. I let go a tirade of threats and accusations that was calculated to inspire even the most lackadaisical Laurel. The results were awful. Absenteeism went up and morale went down. The play remained mediocre, probably no more or less than it would have been without the heated harangue. I was embarrassed and the kids were affected in various ways. Some were hurt, some were angry, and others were incredibly amused.

In retrospect, that experience taught me several things. First, what I learn by observation isn't always what will serve me best. Second, it's not smart to try to be someone or something I'm not. And third, if I must learn by example, there's always the example of the Savior. While he never (to my knowledge) directed a roadshow or managed a corporation, his guidelines for human relations will adapt beautifully to any leadership situation.[1]

I don't intend, in this chapter, to discuss all the "rules" for a successful organization. Leader-follower relationship is only one of many factors that will determine your success or failure. But, if your goal is to prevent burnout in your organization, it is the most important. Whether you measure success in terms of productivity or personal growth, it is imperative that you show respect to everyone under your leadership. That's basic.

Because I'm neither an executive in a corporation nor a professor of management, I'll talk mainly about dealing with others in the church setting—that's something we all have in common. Still, the principles I discuss can be applied to your job, your home, or your community projects.

Say you're a member of an auxiliary presidency, a committee chairman, or home/visiting teacher supervisor. How do you show respect for those for whom you have responsibility? First, go back to the Golden Rule we mentioned earlier. Common courtesy will go a long way. Start with something as simple as the telephone call.

The problem with church work is that there is no specific time set aside to do it, and we are all doing it in whatever fleeting moments we can catch. This, in itself, can tempt us to be disrespectful. It's so easy to disregard other people's schedules because *we* are so busy. For example, it's been a long day and you're finally getting around to doing some planning for a Church activity. Because you're a night person, you think nothing of making a phone call at 10:30 or 11:00 P.M. Don't do it. On the other side of the coin, just because *you're* up and ready to face the world at 6:30 A.M., don't assume that anyone else is.

Each area of the country (world) seems to have its own mores regarding telephone times. I'm tempted to say, as a

---

1. I don't care what you say about righteous indignation, I don't think it's appropriate to compare my uninspired play-cast to the money changers in the temple.

How to Prevent Being the Burner

general rule, unless you have special permission, don't call between 10:00 at night and the time the kids leave for school in the morning. I'm angry if someone calls me late at night; I get violent if someone calls at 7:10 in the morning, when I'm already a few minutes off schedule and I have just stuck the mascara wand in my eye in my rush to get to work on time. When in doubt about people's work and sleep schedules, ask. Find out whether your people *mind* being called late at night, early in the morning, at work (that's taboo in my book), or during the time that most of us eat dinner. And if your call will involve more than a few seconds ask, "Can you talk now or would you like to call me back?"

If there is a rule of thumb I'd like for all of us to remember in doing church work, it's People Before Programs. The truth is, contrary to popular belief, it's not an either-or proposition. In their research, in which they looked at the most successful companies in America, Peters and Waterman[2] found that those companies that topped their list were successful in part because they treated their employees with respect and with a lot of positive reinforcement. They provided challenges which all but guaranteed success for every employee. They gave a lot of pats on the back and few reprimands. They encouraged experimentation. They listened.

While we don't all need the same amount of structure and we can't all handle the same amount of freedom, we *all* thrive on encouragement. As I mentioned in my discussion of kid burnout, many of us believe that if the encouragement doesn't include a chewing out, the pointing out of a mistake, or a nicely couched, "You did this part all right, *but* . . . ," it's not helpful. Research is finally confirming what I've always known at the gut level—that the way to teach is not through criticism. "But," (I hear you!) "it's okay if it's *constructive* criticism." What we're discovering is that "constructive criticism" is an oxymoron. While I'll admit that it's sometimes necessary to call a halt to misguided efforts (which usually come about because we, the leaders, haven't been explicit enough in our directions), criticism is not an effective teaching tool. I'll re-

---

2. Thomas J. Peters and Robert H. Waterman, Jr., *In Search of Excellence: Lessons from America's Best-Run Companies* (New York: Warner Books, 1984).

phrase that. Criticism does teach, but it usually doesn't teach what we *want* to teach, which is usually, in one context or another, success.

Let me illustrate this. If we want to teach success—to a kid, another adult, or anyone—we use positive reinforcement. Positive reinforcement can be anything that appeals to the teachee, and the most lasting reinforcers are the less tangible ones. It's important that you know the person you're dealing with, so you can use the most appropriate reinforcer. For example, if you're trying to teach a difficult kid to be good in Primary and you give him a raisin following every five minutes that he doesn't disrupt, you're on the right track *if* the kid likes raisins. If he doesn't, you're in trouble.

To most adults, positive reinforcement comes in the form of a verbal pat on the back. I guess you could call it praise, but I've never liked that word. The positive feedback has to be sincere, or it won't mean anything. Show excitement about a good idea; show honest appreciation for a job well done. When you're working with someone else, let your positive instincts run wild. But be real. There's a big difference between a respectful pat on the back and a patronizing pat on the *head*.

When we're treated with positive reinforcement, what happens? We learn to succeed. We repeat the kind of behavior that got us the goodies, and we discover that not only does success-producing behavior get us positive strokes from others, but it feels good inside, too. Eventually we learn to be successful with or without the strokes: success becomes its own reward.

On the other hand, what happens when our behavior is shaped through punishment?[3] True, we eventually learn not to make the same dumb mistake again, but guess what else we learn? We learn to shy away from everything *associated* with the punishment, i.e., the leader involved, the auxiliary or committee involved, and, you've all seen examples of this, when the punishment is severe enough or prolonged enough, we even shy away from the organization involved (in this case, the church).

---

3. Punishment, to an adult, can be a reprimand, a disgusted tone of voice, or even intentionally "constructive" criticism.

How to Prevent Being the Burner   117

Before learning theory became the big item in psychology and education, giving positive reinforcement was thought of, by those who'd seen it work, as common sense and effective leadership. Now we have a name for it, behavior modification, and we're wary of using it, especially on other adults. I used to think it was manipulative and that it showed a lack of respect for the individual whose behavior was being modified. Now I think it's great, because I know it *works!* When I know someone is trying to help me to modify my behavior (for the better) I'm delighted. I appreciate the positive reinforcement and I look at it this way. If someone is willing to help me become a better person by issuing recognition at the appropriate time, I'm grateful. It's better than being yelled at.

One of the first things we learn in behavior modification is that the contingency must be clear. In other words, we, as leaders, must outline clearly what we expect. This is where I fell short as a nursery school director. I believe that often the reason we have to criticize is that we are not clear enough about our expectations to begin with, then when they are not met, we have to backtrack. We may be nebulous about our expectations out of laziness or carelessness or, as in my case, we may be exhibiting a misguided desire to allow those under our leadership as much freedom as possible.

I've found that after I've been extremely clear about the outcome I expect, it's good to make suggestions as to ways this can be brought about. This is to satisfy those people who are not self-starters and/or who need a lot of direction. After I have made it clear what is to be done and suggested ways to do it, I like to leave some room for individual inspiration. If I'm working with someone I don't know very well I'll be more protective ("If you think of another way you'd like to do it, I'm open to hear your ideas"). Someone whose dependability has been tried and proven will usually get a casual "These are just suggestions to start with—if you have a better idea, by all means, go with it." Those who I know to be not only dependable but also creative and independent get a simple "I want it to be fabulous. It will be [when] and [where] and you can spend [how much]. Give it the best you've got and call me if you need anything." Start structured and increase freedom as you deem it appropriate. The key is in being sensitive to individual needs. Remember: exacting people are frustrated by an open-ended task. Creative people are stifled by a job which doesn't allow them any personal input.

You're going to have to check up on people, so let them know how and when you intend to do so. If you say, "I'll call you in two weeks to see how things are going," then you can call your [counselor, committee chairman, teacher] in two weeks without it looking like you don't trust him. Being a respectful leader isn't always easy. Having committed yourself to call in two weeks, then one week, then the week before the event, it's important that you follow through.

While I no longer look on the use of positive reinforcement as an underhanded manipulative device, there are some ways that we as Church members manipulate each other that I do find hard to accept. One of these, and one which I believe undermines respect, is The Guilt Trip. For all our teachings against coercion, when some of us get up against the wall we show no mercy for someone who answers no to our requests for help. Granted, there are some people who say no but mean "I really want to, but I'm scared," or "I'm too proud to say yes right off the bat, but keep after me," so it's important that we be prayerful and sensitive, especially with inactive and semi-active members. Still, I think a basic tenet of respect is the willingness to allow others their God-given free agency. While I can handle an occasional "Look, I'm desperate—I've been down the entire ward list and you're my last chance. If you don't take the job I'm going to go into a catatonic state and my visiting teachers will have to take over," I have a *really* hard time with the judgmental pronouncements: "Well, it's *your* eternal salvation!" "It's your light and your bushel," or, after listening to my reasons for not being able to avail myself of the opportunity, "Of course you know that *my* six children are all suffering with chicken pox and mumps simultaneously, and *I* have three other jobs in the church, but if you think you can't handle this little responsibility on top of being PTA president and team mother and other worldly pursuits, well that's fine . . ."

When we are truly committed to the idea of People Before Programs we often find ourselves asking, "Can we really have

How to Prevent Being the Burner

excellence without pressure? without threat? Do we have to sacrifice quality in favor of felicity? Whatever happened to 'tough?' "

There's no doubt that the Church stands for excellence. I know you've all felt the encompassing glow that comes from a superior accomplishment. I'm thoroughly convinced of the divine origin of that feeling. And I know you all know people who achieve great things at work, or who keep their homes like a furniture showroom, but who carry out their church responsibilities with mediocrity. Maybe you've actually *been* one of those people. I know I have. I've always been going to write a chapter or an article on the subject of giving the Church your second best. I wanted to call it "Would You Serve Leftovers on Sunday?"

I've been to Church activities that were so well planned and presented that I was actually spiritually and emotionally lifted just be being there. The joy of the event was dampened only by the fact that I hadn't invited all my nonmember friends to come with me. I've also been to activities that inspired another reaction—evil thoughts like, "I wish I'd stayed home and done my laundry instead," or "Thank goodness I didn't invite so-and-so." Obviously, I prefer the quality activity.

If you allowed yourself to intellectualize you could spend hours arguing the implications of the slogan People Before Programs. Aren't the programs *for* the people? Because we champion all truth and light and everything that is virtuous, lovely, of good report, or praiseworthy, don't we owe ourselves and our people the *best* programs (both literally and figuratively)?

After years of soul-searching and trial and error, I've arrived at this answer. Definitely, when you have to choose between a program and person, choose the person. But if we do it right, guided by a love for people *and* a love for excellence, we shouldn't have to choose. If we lead with love, following the example of the Savior and the promptings of the Spirit (not discounting the access to additional revelation which came with the calling), we should be able to have/give it all. The people we lead are entitled to that warm, transcendent feeling that comes with a great accomplishment. We can teach excellence if we are willing to give our assignment the time and effort it undoubtedly deserves.

Too often we think in terms of getting a job done. Period. We're under too much pressure, not necessarily to achieve, but to finish one project so we can get on to the next. Often we deprive ourselves of the joy of accomplishment, because we spread ourselves too thin. Being thinly spread does not lend itself to depth. Without knowing it we may be encouraging burnout in our co-workers because our own batteries need recharging. The greatest rewards from church work come from the relationships we form with others, from the things we experience together. More meetings isn't the answer, but a higher quality of one-to-one, or -two, or -three contact might be.

I don't have an answer for becoming overcommitted—it's the story of my life. For most of us, whether or not we go to work is not negotiable; neither is whether or not we keep up the house. True, we can simplify, maybe trade in two or three church jobs for one, or take a leave from a community commitment for a while. Or, maybe we can't. Most of us, at one time or another, have to accept the fact that in order to do one thing well we may have to accept less-than-our-best on something else.

I do know that when we magnify our callings the callings cease to be a source of irritation and become instead a source of inspiration. As a leader I challenge you to look at your next assignment in terms of an opportunity to get closer to one or more of your Father in Heaven's children and, as a result, to get closer to your Father in Heaven. Remove your bushel, lengthen your fuse, or otherwise get fired up, because whether you are at work, at home, or at church, the positive effect you have on others will be limited to the warmth and light you generate yourself.

Getting Started 10

There is an old Latter-day Saint saying that goes "some calls are given through inspiration, others through desperation." Bishops' wives are well acquainted with the latter.

Last summer my bishop husband carefully informed me that he was having trouble finding someone to serve as girls' camp counselor from our ward. The conversation eventually progressed to "if we can't find anyone, would you be willing to go?"

There is no part of my being that is tuned in to camping. Why anyone would want to spend four nights in a stuffy tent or cabin, or five days in blazing sun and stifling humidity, has always been beyond me. Oh, I enjoyed camping when I was younger, but that was because girls' camp to me was a week at the MIA Lodge in Brighton, a huge log hotel with real bedrooms and real bathrooms and a real cafeteria, run by paid employees. There we took the two-mile hike with the help of the cool mountain breeze, and the camping experience included a ride on the ski lift and regular trips to the Brighton Store. That was *my* idea of roughing it.

If you think my *mind* was biased against camping, you should have seen my body! There was nothing about my physical self that could possibly have lent itself to the primitive experience our stake had in mind. I'd reached the time of life when one wrong move guaranteed weeks, maybe months, of disc disrepair or sciatic nervousness. Just the thought of a sagging bunk bed triggered the limping response. And what would I wear? While I'd never allow myself to be seen in an *obviously* polyester pair of pants, I had gone to shopping in the women's department, where everything had a little stretch to it. The last time I'd tried to be with it and purchased a pair of jeans had been catastrophic. I'd quickly dismissed the idea of buying the stretch-denim monstrosities in the women's department. If you're going to look with it, halfway measures just don't do the job. I'd also dismissed the idea of a pair of the original Levi's I knew they'd still have at Old Sarge Army Surplus. If I were to be able to hold my head up high in my family of teenagers, I knew I would have to go with the designer brands.

I'd taken my sixteen-year-old shopping with me. She hadn't liked the pants with the pink butterflies on the pocket ("Mom, they went out of style five *years* ago!") nor the ones with the elastic waist ("Mom, get real. Wouldn't it be better to pay full price and have something you could wear in *public?*"). She talked me into trying a pair of tight-legged toreadors with stirrups. It didn't take me long to discount that possibility. Finally we agreed on a pair of ordinary looking jeans with the signature of someone important on the rear.

I'd worn them to the ward picnic with some success. The first part of the evening I'd remained standing—when it had come time to sit, I'd chosen my spot carefully, knowing that I wouldn't be getting up again until it was time to go. When I did get up or down I did so with the utmost care. Then a miracle happened. The pants seemed to mold themselves to my body; they became almost pliable. I grew overconfident, and when they got dirty I washed and dried them. An unredeemable act of destruction, I later discovered. I was never able to get the pants up over my thighs again. I gave them to my daughter, which was probably what she'd had in mind all along.

Getting Started   123

No, I couldn't wear jeans, and my legs were too white and my veins too blue for the Mormon Matron Cutoffs I knew that the younger counselors would be wearing. And there were other reasons I couldn't go to camp, like the rule that no makeup, blow driers, or curling irons were to be allowed on the premises. I was more afraid of pity than of ridicule. Uncomfortable was one thing, but *unattractive*—that was, I believed, adding insult to injury.

Of course I said yes, I'd go, but only on the condition that they couldn't get anyone else. Of course, they couldn't get anyone else. I'd been involved in enough projects that were horrible on the surface and wonderful in the end to know that if I would just do this with the right attitude it would turn out to be one of the all-time great experiences of my life. It did.

I got close to some adorable girls, including my own daughter. My discs kept right on discing and my sciatic nerve was never more serene, in spite of a grueling five-mile hike and a saggy top bunk. The satisfaction I felt during the march up the aisle to receive my master's degree paled in comparison to the bursting sense of pride I felt when I strode to the pulpit to be awarded both my Yearling and my Mountaineer certificates. And the high point of the whole experience was when one of the Beehive girls who had been in my cabin was called on to talk in church, and said that camp had been a wonderful experience for her, and that Sister Day was a real Party Animal.

But there was one thing I didn't conquer. Neither did the co-counselor, nor any of the girls in our cabin, except Kathy, who always came through in a pinch. None of us ever learned to start a fire. With few exceptions, the fire committee for the day would go outside, lay the sticks and logs exactly as it showed in the camp manual, try any number of things (judging from the empty lighter fluid cans I occasionally found around the camp site), and finally come in, discouraged. "Sister Day . . ."

In my cabin were several honor students, several athletes, and some great leaders. My co-counselor and I were no dummies. But none of us could light a fire. We all knew the procedure, we could all go through the motions. But there was some magic that involved getting the flame and the fuel together, in full cooperation, to ensure a lasting blaze. No mean accomplishment. It escaped us.

Kathy and those of you who are seasoned campers are probably either laughing mercilessly or feeling completely baffled that anyone could *not* know how to start a fire. After all, you strike a match, rub stones together, whatever, and it *happens.* Easy for you to say. But some of you may remember that it was difficult for you at first, too. You tried a lot of things a number of times, and some of them worked.

That's how it is with burnout. People who have never experienced burnout have a difficult time believing that such a thing exists, or, having accepted that it does exist, they expect the burnee to recognize it in himself, make the necessary changes, and get rid of it. People who are burned out may have difficulty implementing changes in their lives, even after they have a superficial understanding of what changes must be made. They may lay a lot of logs and sticks and strike several matches before they are able to establish a lasting blaze.

Hopefully by now you will have picked up some common threads, and you understand that while burnout can affect people in several different areas, such as job, marriage, parenting, church job, etc., the causes, symptoms, and remedies for all kinds of burnout are basically the same. Just because you have been working at the same job for years you will not necessarily become burned out. Burnout involves discouragement, a loss of self-esteem, and a loss of self-direction.

Burnout can be caused by lacking balance in your life, having expectations out of line with reality, being guided by a driving force rather than a rational plan, believing that you can't make a difference, or being guided from without rather than from within. While age alone is not sufficient reason for burnout, burnout can be age-related; prime times for episodes of burnout are the teenage years and the midlife years. For many of us, midlife is the time that we are faced with a decision. Do we actually allow ourselves to burn out, and become lonelier and more negative as we grow older, or do we

Getting Started   125

assume responsibility to stir up the eternal flame within us and exert the extra effort it takes to be loving and giving?

I mentioned in an earlier chapter that burnout was reserved for the high achiever, the idealistic person, the one who wants to "make a difference." Nowhere is this more evident than in marriage and parent burnout. People who don't expect much from a relationship may not get much more than they expect, but they don't often find themselves in a tizzie about it. We Latter-day Saints, who grow up with a mental picture of the celestial family, who understand that the most important relationships we will ever have are those within the walls of our homes, and who equate our self-worth with our success as partner and parent, should understand the symptoms of burnout. It is lurking behind every failure or discouragement.

In *Parent Burn-out,* Dr. Joseph Procaccini and Mark Kiefaber divide burnout into four stages.[1] At first the (then potential) victim is full of enthusiasm and high expectations. When rewards don't come as planned, the enthusiasm gradually gives way to doubts and frustration. If the burning-out process is allowed to progress, the doubts and frustration lead to various stages of depression, and finally to total resentment and withdrawal.

This is an accurate picture of the progression of marriage burnout as well as parent burnout. We've all experienced the first two stages, and for most of us life is a constant balancing act, in which we eventually learn to temper our high expectations with reality and to overcome our doubts and frustrations. But when those doubts and frustrations come in extra large doses, or when we take them too personally, or when they hit us at a weak moment, we may not bounce back. We progress to the first stage of depression, and with each progression it becomes more and more difficult to change our direction. Our unhappiness is compounded by a sense of failure. The discrepancy between the angry, increasingly helpless mate or parent we have become and the serene, spiritual fount of

---

1. Dr. Joseph Procaccini and Mark W. Kiefaber, *Parent Burn-out* (New York: Doubleday and Company, 1983).

love and joy we set out to be, is humiliating. Another heaping dose of failure. Enter increasing resentment, and, finally, withdrawal.

The way to win the game is to beat burnout before it reaches its advanced stages, to recognize our potential for burning out and to insulate ourselves against the cold. One way we can do this is to maintain a sense of balance in our lives.

In order to maintain this balance it's important that we pay attention to all areas of our development: spiritual, physical, and social. One author includes financial, and that makes sense if you consider that when we don't have enough money to provide for our needs and those of our families our options become limited and life becomes simply a struggle for survival, with no time or energy to concern ourselves with spiritual or social development. Others include emotional, and I agree that that is a most important area, but I include it in the broad definition of spiritual. I tend to want to include intellectual and/or creative, because I know the joy that comes from learning and accomplishing. Perhaps these could be considered as subheadings, and maybe the subheadings are different for each of us. None of us, however, can function at optimum level without a balance of physical well-being, spiritual development, and healthy relationships with others.

There's another important balance, and that's the balance between what you do for and expect from your significant others (mate and/or kids) and what you do for and expect from yourself. This is a delicate balance, and so easily misinterpreted that I hesitate to approach it for fear of being misunderstood, but it's such an important element in the prevention of burnout that I'll take the risk.

Many women experience marriage burnout because they are unable to find the right balance between submissive and self-directed, between self-sufficient and overly dependent, between selfless and self-effacing. I've heard all kinds of women, from the distraught young mother with eight kids to the professional women who appears to have everything going for her, ask the same question. Where did we get the idea that the way to be a good wife and mother is to eat the burned

Getting Started 127

toast, wear the outdated clothes, and sacrifice the course on educational TV so our kids could watch "The Gong Show?"

I think I'm finally coming to grips with the concept of sacrifice. I used to try to believe that it didn't exist, and when someone would remind me that sacrifice was an important part of the gospel I'd rationalize it away. But the truth won't go away, it just appears in a different context, until we finally catch on to what it's all about.

I've concluded that there is constructive sacrifice and there is destructive sacrifice. Constructive sacrifice is the kind we learn about in church, the kind that makes us strong and obedient and Christlike. Destructive sacrifice is what we do when we let people take advantage of us, when we play the role of "rescuer" or "martyr."

I wouldn't give up the times I stayed up late at night decorating a birthday cake for one of my kids or decorating cookies for a school celebration for anything. I look at our ancient home movies, and see the Halloween costumes I put together with blood, sweat, and tears, risking a knock-down-drag-out with my worst enemy, the sewing machine, and I weep affectionately for good times gone by. I'd do it all again—maybe more often—if I had another chance. To call these acts of motherly love *sacrifice* is to use the term loosely.

The destructive sacrifices we make are those in which we deny ourselves our material, spiritual, or social needs, to satisfy the selfish whims of someone else. The wife who constantly overlooks her need for socialization and recreation and the mother who can never afford a new outfit because her kids have to have the most, the best, and the latest clothes, aren't necessarily adding on to their mansions up on high. More likely they're contributing to the fund for inconsiderate husbands and greedy children and worse, they're burning their own fuel with no means of replenishing it.

Sometimes there is such a fine line between a constructive sacrifice and a destructive one that we can't make the discrimination ourselves—we have to depend on personal revelation. I strongly recommend this tool. In most cases I can judge whether a potential sacrifice is constructive or destructive by the way I feel about the task involved. Usually, when I'm

128   *Coming Up from Down in the Dumps*

called on to make a constructive sacrifice (my experience at
camp is in this category, as is the time I drove rental cars
around Washington, D.C., to raise money for our ward building fund), I feel afraid or even negative about the task to begin
with, but there is usually something, no matter how well
hidden, that tells me: "You've got to do this. You *know* it will
be a great experience if you just let yourself do it." On the
other hand, a potential destructive sacrifice is accompanied by
a feeling of mild irritation and a strong compulsion to be all
things to all people (i.e., Super Mom, Mollie Mormon, or
Helpful Helen.)

Line upon line, I'm learning to reconcile myself to the scrip-
tural references to sacrifice, because I'm beginning to understand them. Take this second mile business, for example.
"Whosoever shall compel thee to go a mile, go with him
twain" (Matthew 5:41). I used to have a *hard* time with this
concept.

The light dawned when I was running, and working on
From Fat to Fit.[2] I noticed that no matter what great shape my
body was in, running the first mile was always a pain. I got
tired. I got discouraged. I wondered whether any positive
effects this punishment might have on my body were really
worth it. But if I could make it to the second mile, I actually
started to enjoy myself. I felt a great sense of accomplishment,
and the task became easier. Don't ask me why; it seemed like
magic.

When I am running, or walking, I am transformed from
daily drudge to profound philosopher. It was while I was
running one morning that I made the comparison. Going the
second mile, as suggested in the scriptures, is similar to running
the second mile, but there is more to it than getting your body
warmed up and deciding that you can do it. When we go the
first (figurative) mile, the one we are compelled to go, we are
the victim. We are only doing what we have been forced to do.
But when we go the second mile we are in control. By going
the second mile we are saying, "I choose to do this for you,"

---

2. Afton, Day,*From Fat to Fit in Four Grueling Months* (Salt Lake City: Bookcraft, 1979).

Getting Started   129

and we are free to add our own personal touches, thus bringing our own talents, our own initiative, and our own intellect into the picture. The second mile is exciting, because it's an extension of ourselves.

That's how I can reconcile our behavior as wives and mothers. I'd never want to be quoted as saying, "Stop doing things for your kids and your husbands—just look out for yourselves." The real joys of family life come from loving and giving, but the giving has to be self-motivated before it can yield positive results.

I've found the same principle to be true at work. When I do only what I'm compelled to do I'm tired and overworked and very resentful toward the compellor. But when I look at the assignment and say, "Okay, how can I really put 'me' into this project?" I end up loving it, and I almost always accomplish something that I'm proud of. I may spend more time and work harder than I would if I were simply to satisfy the bare requirements, but just as I do when running the second mile, I get the energy from some mysterious source, and the otherwise irritating assignment becomes a labor of love.

If you have reached the advanced stages of burnout you may have to focus on giving to yourself before you can get into the joy of giving to others. I've often wondered why this is true, as it seems to contradict all the things we are taught in church and in the scriptures about sacrifice and losing yourself. Oh, every now and then, like in Matthew 22:39, we get a hint that it is okay to take care of ourselves, but my personal belief is that it wasn't intended that we should need to be reminded that our own needs are important. Our spiritual selves knew that when they came to live in our bodies, but most of us have somehow lost sight of the fact that we are worth the trouble.

When you adopt a baby through an agency there are several stages of interviews and home visits. When we adopted our first child we had to be interviewed after we had the baby in our home, and before the adoption was final. At that time the social worker gave me what is now, I realize, some very good advice, although I would have given it in a more general manner. She said: "Promise me that you will take one day out of every week for yourself. Get a sitter, or trade days with a friend, but somehow, arrange some time for yourself."

At the time I thought she was completely out of touch with my needs. Of course I promised, because I wanted to keep the baby, but getting out of the house once a week was the furthest thing from my mind. I had waited nearly five years for that baby, and I wanted to spend time with *him*.

At that particular time I really didn't need that advice, nor did I in the immediate years to come. I had enough occasions to leave my kids, on church assignments or social events, that they learned to stay with baby-sitters, and I had everything I wanted from life. But as time went on I've discovered that that social worker knew what she was saying. I didn't need time away then, but what I did need was to remember how it felt to give to myself, because for me, as is inevitable for all of us, there did come a time in my life when I needed to give myself some tender loving care, and by that time I had forgotten how. My scales had tipped too far on the side of efficiency, expediency, and exhaustion. It was easier for me to complain of tiredness, anger, and depression than to lift the phone and arrange for an uplifting evening with a friend.

Maintaining balance is important in missionary work, too. I asked Elder Gerald Day,[3] former president of the Chile, Vina del Mar, Mission, what suggestions he would offer to prevent missionary burnout. Repeatedly he said, "Follow the program."

You may have guessed by now that I am drawn to off-the-wall answers and esoteric insights. I was a little disappointed when this man, whom I knew to be brilliant and perceptive, gave such a predictable reply. Of course I believe in obedience, but I appreciated it when he expounded. The program, he explained, is designed to provide balance. It attends to the missionary's spiritual development, physical and emotional well-being, and social and recreational needs. President Wayne A.

---

3. Elder Day is presently Regional Representative to the Dominican Republic and Dean of the College of Management at the Georgia Institute of Technology (Georgia Tech). Yes, we are related.

Getting Started   *131*

Mineer, president of the Georgia, Atlanta, Mission, agreed wholeheartedly. When a missionary neglects any one of the aforementioned areas, there is a potential for problems.

The missionary most susceptible to burnout, Elder Day suggested, is the one who takes himself[4] too seriously. President Mineer was quick to add that this, by no means, should imply that it was possible to take The Work too seriously. This idea brings forth all kinds of insights and inspirations I've had that illustrate the paradox involved in the necessity of (forgive my colloquialism) hanging loose while holding tightly to the iron rod.

My testimony of hanging loose is, appropriately, based on a lot of random, seemingly unrelated experiences. First, observation. It never ceases to amaze me to discover that the real spiritual leaders of the Church, from those in high positions down to those working at the ward level who perform miracles among the youth or their home/visiting teaching families, are not the straight-laced, fuddy-duddy types I thought they would be.

I first recognized the easy, unaffected warmth I'm talking about when I, as a twelve-year-old, was introduced to President David O. McKay. I was overcome with the recognition of the same unmistakable quality as I listened to Dr. James Mason, then our stake president, being released to take charge of the Church Medical Services, and now a Regional Representative for the Church and director of the Communicable Disease Center in Atlanta. I knew, in the presence of these men, that what I was feeling was their depth of spirituality. My reaction to this was a lump in my throat and tears in my eyes.

While the "spiritual giants" I have observed are intensely earnest in their commitment to the gospel, often their spirituality has come through in humor, fun, and warmth. I've felt comfortable in their presence. I've had the impression I've described as I've met with the mission presidents and their

---

4. Again, by assigning the male gender to this discussion on missionary work, I am definitely not pretending that all missionaries are, or by any means should be, men. I'm just trying to save my syntax.

families who have served in our area, and the president and matron of our Atlanta temple. I have yet to meet an uptight, truly spiritual person.

The message also came through personal revelation. Several years ago I was nursing a grudge or plotting some revenge for a personal injury, the nature of which escapes me just now, when the Spirit said, "What you need to do is to learn to hang loose." I don't wish to attribute slang expressions to the Spirit; what I believe happens is that he puts the conceptual message in our minds and we interpret it into language.

I was surprised at this message, because I had *certainly* never associated "hanging loose" with living the gospel. But the message was too strong to be rationalized away, and it has since been confirmed many times in a variety of ways. I now know that the state I think of as hanging loose is the same state the Christian world calls "letting go," and it has to do with faith, trust, unconditional love, and un-self-conscious confidence. At times I think that it will be about as easy for me to give up stewing and worrying as it was for the rich man to give what he had to the poor (Matthew 19). Hanging loose would mean letting go of fears, of worries, of grudges, and hurt feelings—much of the intrigue that makes my life exciting. And for what? Peace, serenity, eternal life.

It's easy to see why the missionary who learns not to take himself too seriously has an advantage over the one who agonizes over everything. Look at the things you missionaries are called on to do, for example. First, *get along with a large assortment of companions,* some of whom, it seems, were called for the express purpose of making your life difficult. Second, *love the people,* who may, collectively, be as diametrically opposed to what you've always thought of as "acceptable" as night is to day. And third, *work with the members,* some of whom are guaranteed, by the law of probability, to be completely tactless, thoroughly unexemplary, or totally uncooperative.

Presidents Mineer and Day both agreed that those missionaries who had problems (whether the problems were called burnout, fallout, or trunkiness) were those who either never

Getting Started   133

learned to depend on the Spirit or those who, after several successes, started to take success for granted and (probably unconsciously) made the decision to make it on their own. I've heard so many returned missionaries tell of the hopelessness and frustration they experienced before they learned to rely on the Spirit that, I guess, if there were only one thing I could teach the future missionaries in my family, this would be it. The key to not only a productive mission, but a happy one (and from what I understand, during the course of two years "happy" runs the gamut from "tolerable" on one end of the continuum to "ecstatic" on the other) is an ongoing working relationship with the Holy Ghost.

How is this achieved? Through scripture study and prayer, of course. But also, suggested President Mineer, by meeting new people, by trying new things, by implementing new plans, and by applying new solutions to old problems. Also by "going back to square one" if you see yourself becoming stale or self-centered. Elder Day expounded on the idea of novelty. "Missionary work should not be mechanical. When you live by the Spirit," he says, "often you are amazed at the inspiration you receive. Spirit-oriented missionaries often find success through unconventional (but not *unallowable*) means."

If you see some symptoms of burnout in yourself or in someone you love, and the answer to the question, "Where do I start?" hasn't reached out and grabbed you, hang on. Let the information in this book incubate. It may take weeks, even months, before you can relate to a principle or a practice that actually applies to you. Many of us have very protective minds, and we are resistant to confrontation and change. Only as we pray for insight and prove our readiness to accept it will we be given the understanding we need.

To sum it all up, here are some hints for overcoming burnout:

1. *Try tracing your burnout to its source.* If your burnout has since generalized, this may take some thought, but it will be easier to overcome if you know where it started. What happened to you just before your life started going downhill? Did

you change jobs? Have triplets? Lose a loved one? Pinpointing a specific event or series of events will give you a place to start working.

2. *Re-examine your life-style.* Have you lost the balance between the spiritual, physical, and social areas of your life? Are you slighting one area of development in favor of another? Is it all work and no play?

3. *Get in touch with your inner/spiritual self,* or, in other words, "Get right with God."

4. *Learn not to expect rewards from outside yourself.* It's okay to *enjoy* them, when they come, but don't base your life on them.

5. *Discover recreation for its own sake.*

6. *Cultivate close relationships with others.*

7. *Realize that you are responsible for your own self-esteem,* and work to acquire a quiet confidence that is based on you as a Child of God, and not on your achievements.

8. *Count your blessings,* or, in other words, learn to dwell on the positives in your life.

Keep at it; it's worth it. One of these days you'll be stricken with the realization that you are walking in the light again, and the thrill will be worth all the effort. "Light" and "warmth" signify all that is right and true, while "darkness" and "cold" stand for the opposite extreme. At the risk of being an over-protective author, may I remind you to remember who you are and what you represent, and live accordingly.